MODERN MOTOR BIKES
IN COLOUR

MODERN MOTOR BIKES
IN COLOUR

by

Laurie Caddell

Colour Photography

by

JASPER SPENCER-SMITH

BLANDFORD PRESS

POOLE DORSET

First published in 1979
by Blandford Press Ltd,
Link House, West Street, Poole, Dorset BH15 1LL

© *Blandford Press Ltd 1979*
ISBN 0 7137 0989 8

British Library Cataloguing in Publication Data

Caddell, Laurie
  Modern motor bikes in colour.
  1. Motorcycles
  I. Title
  629.22'75   TL440

Colour Plates by Cox & Wyman, Fakenham
Printed and bound in Great Britain by
Butler & Tanner Ltd,
Frome and London

CONTENTS

ACKNOWLEDGEMENTS

Laurie Caddell and Jasper Spencer-Smith wish to thank the following companies for making available motor cycles from their stock for photography:

Boscombe Motor Cycle Centre, Bournemouth, Dorset;
Etna Motor Cycles, Parkstone, Dorset;
Horswill Motor Cycles, Bournemouth, Dorset;
Ray Fisher Motor Cycles, Christchurch, Dorset;
Motor Cycle City, Farnborough, Hampshire;
Station Garage, Taplow, Buckinghamshire;
Rye's Motor Cycles, Southampton;
Three Cross Motor Cycles, Verwood, Dorset;
Peter Williams Motor Cycles, Southampton, and
Quasar Motor Cycles, Staple Hill, Bristol.

TOWARDS THE MODERN BIKE AND BEYOND

We are in the late 1970s enjoying a boom period in motor cycling with companies offering a bewildering array of machines in all shapes and sizes with as much or as little advanced technology built in as you could wish. You could want a push-button monster with a sewing-machine-smooth multi-cylinder engine producing a seemingly endless supply of power and speed, or be more content with a big single or twin on which you can feel each and every power stroke and which needs to be given constant attention just to be kept in running order. Whatever, the choice is there, and you can rest happy in the knowledge that running a bike is a whole lot more than having a cheap form of transport at hand, for being out there with the elements and having consciously to be aware of and make allowances for other more forgetful road users gives an almost primeval pioneering spirit to the rider. Instead of getting in a car and locking yourself away, you are almost starting on a new adventure each time you ride off, and you are right there with the delights, and sometimes dangers, just a few engine revolutions away. It is something which has not changed and, indeed, will never change no matter how advanced motor cycles become.

Far from being advanced, man's first attempts at powered two-wheelers were very sorry affairs, aided not at all by the only power system available at the time, namely the steam engine. It is hard to imagine what it was like travelling over the rutted and rock-strewn tracks on a solid-wheeled, solid-framed bike with a fiery boiler bubbling and ready to explode at any moment tucked behind the motor cyclist's back. Luckily, these monsters, which were envisaged around the 1850s and which, it was claimed, ran a few years later, did not catch on and it was not until the arrival of the internal-combustion engine that man had the chance to increase his mortality rate on two wheels on the road.

As with most things automotive, there is a great deal of conjecture as to who actually built the first petrol-powered cycle, although it would be fair to say that the two main contenders are Gottlieb Daimler and Edward Butler, whose designs saw the light of day in 1885 and 1884, respectively. What is true is that their initial designs sparked off many ideas around the 'motor cycle' and,

I

although diversified at times, a pattern was to appear. Hilderbrand & Wolfmüller first put a bike into production, in 1894, while Werner in 1901 set the style for its design with a machine of push-bike proportions with the engine and power take-off point where the pedals would normally be. Just to make sure that nobody would lay claim to the idea in later years, Holden built several four-cylinder bikes, the first of which appeared in 1897. To help the cycle manufacturer who could not run to the expense of building his own motors, Comte Albert de Dion and Georges Bouton offered for sale the first proprietary engines to clip on to frames. So, the stage was set and the industry had established designs, a power unit that was becoming ever more powerful and reliable and a world wanting to experience the self-propelled machine. The car was there, too, but that would soon become too complex and even further out of the reach of the pockets of the ordinary man.

In the years to come, the motor cycle industry would survive two world wars, countless slumps and market depressions to arrive in the 1970s as one of the growing and more prosperous industries. Indeed, with the car being the prime target of attack for conservationalists and environmentalists, the bike with its inherent economy advantages was to become ever more popular.

The main reason for the biking renaissance of the 1960s and '70s has been the growth of the Japanese industry since World War II and its ability in making drawing-room dreams a production reality. Considering Japan's position in 1946, it is quite remarkable that by the early 1970s their bike exports would be several million units. In the year after the war, there was a grand total of 1603 civilian motor cycles registered there and the companies that survived mostly relied on imported engines or cribbed designs at best. Why did the revolution start in Japan which had previously had such a low standard of living? It is said that necessity is the mother of invention and, although they didn't invent the motor cycle, they did have the necessity for cheap transport when their rail systems and bus services were in tatters. The ordinary man could fit a suitable power unit to his push bike and, if it worked, could do another for a friend; so, from nowhere, small factories started to spring up. Many, of course, would sink without trace, but others would soldier on, and in a five-year period from 1949, production in Japan increased from around 1500 units to well over 100,000 with some 80 manufacturers involved. Import blocks on foreign machinery made sure that the industry would survive, while a desire to wage war on western bikes from both the showroom and racetrack impassioned the Japanese by no small amount.

However many machines they produced it did not matter to the rest of the world, for the quality did not match up to the quantity, as most were little more than dated autocyles. It was obvious that only the fittest were to survive if the country was to be a threat to Italy, Great Gritain, Germany and America. Racing was to improve the breed, as a series of events at a circuit called Asama attracted the interests of the major manufacturers, many of whom are long forgotten in Japan and have hardly even been heard of outside: Cabton, DSK, Marusho, Tsubasa and Rikuo are examples. Others had more ingenuity, were more successful and so succeeded: Meguro were bought up by Kawasaki Aircraft in 1964, as the aviation company decided to jump on the bike bandwagon; SJK renamed as Suzuki; musical instrument maker Yamaha tried bikes, too, and indeed still use their three-tuning-fork emblem on their machines; Honda were most successful at Asama and even debuted a four-cylinder there in 1959. They had a reason for being the best : Sochiro Honda himself had been to Europe and seen the British and Italian machinery lapping at phenomenal speeds on the Isle of Man ; he just had to go back and prove that he could do better.

By the early 1960s, the feelers had been put out and soon everybody was to take notice of the now exotic machinery that boasted such funny Oriental names and which sounded like nothing on earth. It just needed a little money to tempt the best European riders on to the bikes and the battle would be won, for the ordinary biker would relate to it all and want to be part of it. He could afford the mopeds and small bikes that shared the name with the race winners, where a few years earlier the purchase of a Gilera, Moto Guzzi, MV Agusta or even Norton might have been out of the question.

How did other countries react to the invasion? Germany, who had built some 200,000 bikes in the year just before the war, was in the same position as Japan, but somehow did not have the passion or the absolute need to be so inventive, and so carried on almost

3

from where they left off. Their major manufacturer, BMW, picked up its old design, modified it and carried on, right to where they are today with basically the same bike. The great Depression had killed most of America's industry years before the war, anyway, leaving Indian and Harley-Davidson as the major suppliers. Their bikes were also in a different class. A Harley owner would consider no other bike and, although no-one in America would try and stem the rush of imports, no-one would stop buying their own great American freedom machine, either.

Italy suffered at the hands of Japan, but the glory on the race tracks in the 1950s would be enough to see the manufacturers through into the late 1960s and early 1970s, and even if there was to be a further crisis, there would still be enthusiasm and money ready to bail out. The major figure in the Italian industry has been the Argentinian Alejandro de Tomaso. One time Vice President of Ford in America, he travelled to Italy and almost single handed got things running when times looked bleak. He may have made enemies and, indeed, the country is split down the middle with people for and against him, but he has kept many names alive and more importantly made them prosperous. Benelli and Moto Guzzi were taken over and, when MV were about to transfer production to the Ducati factory who themselves were in danger of folding, it was de Tomaso who expressed interest in offering a helping hand. Italy cannot compete with Japan with production of full size motor cycles, so they build cheap mopeds for the masses (just like France who prosper in this field, too) and make primarily sporting bikes which are as charismatic as they are nimble.

The true casualty is, of course, Great Britain who at one time produced bikes the envy of the world. Its industries' death, however, is as much suicide as murder for it did not adapt when the need arose. By the time the world was beginning to accept the multi-cylinder bike as a road machine and not just a freak racer, the British industry was still quite content with resting on its parallel-twin laurels. Vincent, whose machines were legends even before they left the production line, were forced out when the late 1950s dictated a move to smaller less grandiose bikes, and if they could go down anybody could. By the time that BSA-Triumph decided to tack on an extra cylinder to their 500 twin it was too late. Precede the big 750 Honda it may have done, but the Trident was for its ingenuity still no more than one-and-a-half 500 twins in the eyes of most. The industry in Britain even at this time was perhaps starry eyed because the Americans who couldn't afford Harleys might just accept a Bonny or Commando instead, but what was the point of a few enthusiastic exports to the USA when the home market was crying out for something British that would compete with the ever-growing Japanese tide? By the time NVT was producing Easy-Rider mopeds to make a basis for their more advanced projects, it may have been too late. Small specialist manufacturers continued to prove that it was not lack of sound design that was to blame, while even NVT had a range of machines on the drawing board that in metal would have had few peers. That was where the difference lay, however, between Britain and Japan.

The future may hold few surprises and will surely see the Japanese dominance remain if not increase. Unlike the car industry where everyone can offer opposition, the bikes have few rivals and so a block on that country's exports is out of the question, for there would be nothing with which to fill the void. It is left to the rest of the world to catch up slowly if at all possible, while the companies involved might just decide that status quo has been reached and that they are all happy producing their separate wares. The burden then falls on the Japanese industry to keep the potential buyers' attention and continue to build bikes that grow in specification and standards of equipment each and every year.

A great deal of racing-bike technology goes into the road machines of today, a far greater amount than the car industry can boast. For example, strip the body off an MV Agusta and it will take a trained eye to tell the difference between a racing and road version. Inside the engine, too, there is a great deal of similarity. Yamahas have dominated the 250 and 350cc classes of Grand Prix racing for many years now with bikes that are strikingly similar to their roadsters in the engine department, with the main modification being the adoption of water cooling. The GT750 Suzuki was identical almost to that company's superbike racers and the latest 650, 750, 900 and 1000cc Hondas have engines which were developed from their Formula One and Endurance Racer machines. More generally, the disc brake since its appearance on the circuits has prompted a braking revolution on road bikes, pioneered by Bridgstone and mass produced by Honda; gas dampers and forks are becoming increasingly popular, with the GS1000 Suzuki the first to exploit the system developed on Grand Prix bikes; alloy wheels which offer the advantages of lighter weight and greater strength than the spoked variety transformed racing and are now transforming the appearance and roadworthiness of our street machines; and tyres are perhaps the most forgotten components in the motor cycle make up. However, the tyre technician is the man on whom the greatest responsibility falls, and his lessons learnt on the racing circuits with different mixes and compounds, sizes and tread patterns will be passed on to the road rider who can be sure that his tyres will work well in conditions wet or dry and will last longer and be more resistant to punctures and blow outs.

It is surprising that in all the advanced technology that goes into engine, brake and tyre design, few people seem particularly bothered with the modern motor bike's biggest drawback: its frame. Even the best GP machinery to grace the tracks in the late 1970s can boast little more than a mangled conglomeration of tubing that would make car designers, aircraft engineers and metallurgists alike shudder in disbelief. These high-performance racers are running around with frames that are little more than sturdy push-bike designs and, indeed, not far removed from that first Werner. The race engineers seem content to increase their bikes' performances by having stickier tyres and more powerful engines with that old standby of welding some bracing struts to the chassis if the power or roadholding gets too much and affects handling.

There are, of course, exceptions to this general trend, but it is left up to the individuals who go endurance racing to dabble with ideas like hub-centre or kingpin steering, low-mounted fuel tanks and scientific frame design. There have been many attempts at the monocoque bike, the Norton racer being a major example, while Bimota have at least proved that a sound spine design can give a standard racer a leading edge, Cecotto's Yamahas and Villa's Harley-Davidsons being proof of this. Bimota do build road bikes but only in such small numbers as to cater for the rich enthusiast, while the rest of roadster production relies mainly on chassis inferior to the not-so-great race bikes. Certain Japanese bikes of the late 1960s and early 1970s ably demonstrated that having a great deal of power in a weak frame is only acceptable if you have the flat surface and open spaces of a track to experiment and perhaps a set of tyres that would hold the plot together. If you had a 'stroker' Kawasaki or the like and tried to use its performance on the swings and roundabouts of the country you could find that under certain conditions the bike felt strangely articulated or spongy. You may have realised this after a nasty 'tank slapper' which sent you cursing or sent you tumbling. Either way, you would have had first-hand experience of antiquated frame design. A case of modern motor bikes being not so modern.

So in the end a manufacturer will come up with an acceptable mix for a bike they wish to market: the engine will be there, so will the frame (however good) and all the running gear. That will be only the start, however, for the appearance of a machine is these days just as important.

Firstly, alloy wheels must be considered because the public has decided that spokes are old fashioned and out. If alloy wheels are going to be too expensive be like Honda and produce a Comstar with an alloy rim and steel spokes that look the part; or be like Yamaha with their XS1100 and have a complete cast iron wheel. Disc brakes are a must of course because they look so much neater than drums, even if few disc-braked roadsters have come near to matching the performance of the drum units fitted to the Vincent Black Shadow, for example. The drum fitted at the back of the CX500 Honda in its Comstar wheel looks attractive as does the conical brake set up used by Campagnolo in their alloy wheel and seen on the race tracks with certain Harley-Davidsons, but the disc is here to stay, with slots, cross drillings, sintered steel pads, anti-lock devices and all. Then there are the instruments that have to be there even if they are given little attention when the bike is in motion. The more gauges, dials and idiot lights the better. Of course, they are useful, but the designer has to cater more for aesthetics than practicality.

The bike's bodywork is probably the biggest headache of all for from a time when machines were virtually identical, the last few years has seen clever design staff jiggle around with the admittedly small components to produce finished machines which look different from one another, with some good and some bad. Even Kawasaki who added a little tail-fairing cum cubby hole to their bikes of the late 1960s could not have foreseen that virtually every bike produced a few years later would have a similar design of tail piece as a matter of course.

Honda were to learn the biggest lesson with their Dream series 250 and 400 models that were met with the greatest apathy when presented to an unsuspecting market. The bike that hastily replaced it, the Super Dream, was basically the same underneath the new clothes, but the different tank, side panels and tail was enough to make a great deal of difference.

Even with the eager buyer apparently catered for, there is still much to be done, for a bike that suits the builder and the buyer had these days to cater for somebody else: the man who works out the regulations covering lighting; specifications for different ages of rider; noise; and, most importantly, exhaust emissions. The lights are the least of his problems for a powerful and correctly adjusted system will suffice except in the few areas where 'daylight headlights' are compulsory. Now that Great Britain does not require its moped riders to be able to give their machines pedal assistance, restrictors to make them travel at 30mph or less are the only worry. A decent exhaust that is not too restrictive will make sure that noise isn't a great problem, but the emission regulations and controls could take as much time sorting out as the rest of the bike altogether.

Environmentalists and ecologists have all but killed off the two-stroke machine and even though it continues to dominate on the race tracks and has no competitor to oust it, its days on the road are all but numbered except for the smallest of bikes which use so little fuel that they hardly matter. Not that the four-stroke engine has escaped completely, although it is not frowned upon as much as similar units in cars. The effect of catalytic converters, stratified-charge engines and using low-octane fuel has drastically cut the performance of cars sold in America, for example, and the road performance of machines there will never ever reach the peak that was achieved in the mid 1960s. The motor cycle industry has been able to cope with the small demands imposed on them and, roughly speaking, power has dropped on larger bikes by just a couple of horsepower since emission controls were brought in. Kawasaki, for example, have on all their four-strokes a positive crankcase breathing system which recycles blow-by gases and reduces hydrocarbon exhaust emission by, they say, up to 40%. The toll on power is minor, and the engineers can get back what has been taken away by steady development of combustion chamber design. 5mph bumpers and energy-absorbing structures and steering columns have yet to be specified for motor cycles, so there at least with a bit of common sense the designer is allowed free rein.

There it is: the new bike is on the road where it can join the countless others and all that has to be done is for a salesman to attract the customer, which if the sums have been done correctly, should be as simple as can be. What does the rider choose, though, and what sort of bike does he want? Engine size ranges from around 50cc to almost 1400cc; top speed ranges from 25mph to around 150mph; while fuel consumption varies from about 300mpg for a 'powered push bike' to under 30mpg for a multi-cylinder sports machine.

Obviously, the first place to look if you want a good performer with lots of reliability is the Japanese manufacturers. Bikes that do better than them cost a lot more and the differences will probably only be noticeable in the uppermost ranges of performance where even the quickest of riders will be for just a few per cent of the time he is in the saddle. Firstly, decide how much or little performance you want and whether your bike will be used mostly for commuting a few miles to work, touring across continents or purely for fun at the weekend. Even learner machines of up to 250cc can be placed in those three categories, so the choice is very large indeed. A two-stroke bike for a given capacity will usually have more power and so a greater performance than a four-stroke; will be more sensitive to the throttle; have a narrower power band (which will make it necessary to keep the motor running quicker for the extra zip) and be thirstier and more temperamental in traffic with its fouling sparking plugs.

It will also be easier to maintain due to its simple construction, and will be smoother than a four-stroke of the same configuration, although will be tiresome on long journeys. Having decided what type of engine is most suitable, you can then figure out how many cylinders you need. A small single will be adequate for mopeds and lightweight but further up the scale the choice will usually be 'two cylinders or more'? The latest batch of counter-balanced twins are quite smooth indeed and unless used at the top of their rev ranges will not cause too many vibration and hence fatigue problems . . . for bike or rider. There is a considerable weight saving with just two cylinders while a bike thus equipped will be narrower and therefore feel easier to manoeuvre than a multi. Next up is the three-cylinder machine which is the least popular configuration of all. Balance of the engine, either primary or secondary, is in between that of a two- or four-cylinder, so the 'three' is something of a compromise unit altogether. A four-cylinder is the most popular design for larger bikes where balance, and therefore vibration, is a big problem. These engines offer great smoothness and power and are usually so understressed that reliability is a problem that rarely crops up. The next, and so far final, step up is the six-cylinder engine which is the smoothest of all and the most powerful, but the problem arises of their enormous width. Not only does it hinder cornering (as the crankcase is likely to touch the ground first), but a mass of engine offered to penetrate air at anything up to 140mph does not do the job that efficiently.

Once you have decided what power unit is needed it is only left to the extras on top that one manufacturer produces that another doesn't and vice versa. Touring or racing style does not matter a great deal, for most of what is offered from Japan is a compromise that will suit no rider perfectly but every rider adequately.

Maybe something common and even bland to a degree is not for you, and you may need something more expensive but a little more sporting. Then the obvious market to turn to is the Italian. Obviously, their output is much smaller than Japan's but they have machines as varied and in all cases have an edge in performance on the road if not on paper. Also in all cases, reliability will be a little less and the finish will be a little or a lot poorer, but a hand-made machine may have a little more character for you than one rolling off a production line. Apart from Japan and Italy, few other countries market their machines on a wide basis, and few bikes are available to the mass market. The exceptions are the German BMW and the American Harley-Davidsons, although these bikes are unique and unlikely to have no competitors in their respective owners' eyes. The communist bloc countries market machines like Cossacks, Jawas, CZs and MZs, but it would be fair to say more at the economy end of the range. Generally speaking, though, the other countries' manufacturers bother little with exports and make their way selling machines specifically suited to the needs of the local populous. In the past ten years or so, road bikes have reached Britain from places like Mexico, Portugal, India and Spain, but never to such an extent that they have greatly affected sales of bikes imported in larger quantities.

The smaller competition bike market knows no such boundaries, though, and one can readily buy a Swedish Husqvarna, Spanish Bultaco, Austrian KTM or American Rokon, for example.

Nowadays, modern bikes are very reliable and makers are able to offer warranties on them without risking a great deal of money. Although for off-road competition bikes it is really a matter of personal discussion regarding specific complaints and whether the bike has gone wrong on its own or been maltreated in any way, a guarantee will generally include free parts and labour for six months to a year, sometimes with a specified mileage or sometimes unlimited.

The choice of bikes is enormous, the quality with very few exceptions is excellent, but what can be expected in years to come and how will the motor bike develop from here?

One may think that engine design has just about reached a peak with bikes like the XS1100 Yamaha, CBX Honda and Z1300 Kawasaki around, but you can guarantee that development of more complex and even faster machines will continue for some time. As far as new concepts of power unit are concerned, the bike industry will follow a few steps behind that of the car. Suzuki and DKW/Hercules got their fingers burnt with the Wankel, while Yamaha opted out of their plans for rotary bikes just in time. NVT seem convinced that the idea is still worthy of time and money, but their bike is meant to be a no-compromise low-volume production sportster aimed at those to whom fuel consumption will be of little consequence. For the mass market, however, the Wankel as yet is not a practical proposition and, until a breakthrough with rotor-tip reliability and fuel consumption problems have been achieved in cars, there will be no revolution of the sort with two wheelers.

Across-the-frame engines, too, have gone as far as is practical with the Benelli Sei, Z1300 Kawasaki and Honda CBX, and even Honda had to pull out all the stops with their design ingenuity to make their six narrow enough not to furrow the tarmac every time it was laid over in a corner. It will be a brave and foolish man who presents his superiors with plans for a straight-eight, however extravagant and publicity magnetising it will be. The future is based on the vee-configuration unit in multiple-cylinder guise, longitudinal for shaft drive, as is sensible, or across the frame, which is better suited for sports bikes that cannot afford the complication or added weight of the shaft. An across the frame vee engine canted forwards may be adequately cooled by air, but the chances are that liquid cooling will be increasingly utilised, for as well as leaving the designer a free hand at its location, it will allow higher combustion chamber temperatures to be attained without the added problem of heat dissipation at lower speeds and allow cylinders to be closer together. That such an engine will seem smoother and be quieter are added bonuses.

The turbocharger is another key to the future for, although it has been used in racing now on and off since the 1930s, only recently has it been thought necessary for roadsters. In recent years, various small tuning companies have been experimenting with turbo-charged 750s and 1000s, while Kawasaki took the major step of introducing a turbo bike through their 1000-odd dealerships in America to be an intermediary until they could launch their competitor to the CBX. Making the quickest of bikes quicker is of more novelty value than anything else when it comes to supercharging, for the real future lies with the smaller bikes. For example, a 350 or 500cc machine with a turbo could rival present-day 750s or 1000s when the need arises, while still being economical and tractable for town use, The necessarily lower compression ratio would ensure better fuel consumption than a normally aspirated competitor (although at the loss of performance bite), while being much quicker when the performance is needed. Dropping down a couple of gears and opening the throttle wide would ensure the complete transformation. A move to fuel injection would be advisable with turbos.

As far as the transmission is concerned, the simple and efficient manual unit is likely to be with us as long as the bike itself. The automatic box is useful for touring and about-town work and most riders will find them strangely addictive, but bikes so equipped with their higher fuel consumption and lower performance are completely opposite to what motor cycling is about for most people. The 750 Hondamatic and 1000cc Convert Moto Guzzi have adequate performances and are passable, but for anything smaller like the 400cc Honda Dream which has trouble keeping up with small cars in a straight line, the future must seem bleak. The shaft drive system is becoming more and more popular as bikes get bigger and put greater demands on chains. Nowadays, as Yamaha, Honda and MV have proved, such a system does not have to be too ponderous and cumbersome in operation, even though it can never be as smooth and as slick as the chain.

Braking is an area where there has recently been a lot of development with Moto Guzzi pioneering the way with their integral system, whereby the front and rear systems are linked mechancially. Kawasaki were next to join the fray with their range being transformed with the adoption of sintered-steel pads. Anti-lock systems will start to be seen on bikes in the near future, too. Having disc brakes which work in the wet is only now becoming something for the everyday rider and not just a luxury for those who could afford machines with cast-iron discs.

It has taken the Japanese industry a long time to discover that their frames leave a lot to be desired in terms of structural rigidity, but slowly they are making them adequate if not brilliant. Having a chassis made of straight tubing with triangulated joints is an ideal which cannot be achieved on a bike with a large engine, but development on those lines is taking place, with the specialist manufacturers leading the way. A move to any radical form of frame or chassis is, if at all, a long way away off unless again someone can show in practical terms that the efforts to new goals are that significant, or more importantly in this commercial world, to be appreciated by every rider. Some companies are considering monocoques, but are loath to be the first to try one out with the public.

The one other major advancement of the future will be in the area of bodywork, for the rider of today who wishes to travel great distances demands some form of protection from the elements that special clothing alone cannot ensure.

Things will develop along the lines of the immaculate fairing fitted to the RS BMW which has proved so popular. Yamaha have a full fairing as an option on their XS1100 which is interesting in that the top half swivels with the bars, while the lower part, armed with extra lighting, is rigidly mounted. Soon, manufacturers will realise that they can break in on the specialist manufacturers who make a living out of building fairings and produce their own, specifically designed for each model. A full roof, like that of the revolutionary Quasar, may be seen on an ordinary roadster, but the trend will probably stop at efficient dolphin or even dustbin designs.

In the course of less than a hundred years, the motor bike has advanced from a slow and fragile push-bike design that could be outrun by even the unfittest of men to the modern motor bike of today that has the pace of a missile being fired. The future may bring a lot more advancement but, even if one day there will be offered a turbocharged twin-rotor Wankel bike with automatic transmission, shaft drive, gyroscopic balancers, to ensure the bike stayed upright at rest, and a full fairing with built-in heater and sound system, you can still bet your last penny that somewhere there will still be a single-cylinder bike with kickstarter on offer with people queuing up to buy it just to sample the basic pleasures motor biking can give.

1 BENELLI 250CE

The Italian firm of Benelli produce two completely different 250 motor cycles, the cheaper and less glamorous one being their 250CE. The 250CE is a two-stroke, twin-cylinder bike which follows the layout of the popular Japanese bikes in the quarter litre class. With a 56mm bore and 47mm stroke, the engine actually displaces 231cc from which is extracted 30bhp at 8000rpm. This power gives the small Benelli a top speed of 90mph and a fuel consumption of 45mpg. Again, as is usual with Japanese machines, a five-speed gearbox with left-foot change is utilised. The frame of the bike is of duplex design and the suspension is conventional in every sense. However, the whole outfit is very taut and well designed, so that the handling and roadholding are of the highest order. One failing of the machine is that it still needs to be fed with petroil mixture instead of the more usual self-mixing set up with separate tanks for petrol and oil.

The finish and appearance is not quite up to the example set by Japanese manufacturers, so the bike misses on this score also. Interestingly, two models of the Benelli 250CE are manufactured, one with drum brakes front and rear and one with a front disc. Although the disc version is considerably more expensive, it is not as effective as the drum in the wet.

Also, if you are not keen on the Benelli name, you can have an identical bike with the Moto Guzzi badges on, as they are made at the same factory.

2 BENELLI 250/4

In a completely different sector of the market to its two-stroke stablemate is the Benelli 250/4 which is, as its name suggests, a four-cylinder bike of approximately 250cc. Like the larger six-cylinder 750 Sei, the 250/4 is an undeniably extravagant bike and that is something which is reflected in its astronomical price, a figure which is almost twice that asked for the CE Benelli. It is not in performance where the four-stroke four has an advantage for, with 26.5bhp and a top speed of just on 90mph, the CE gives nothing away at all. What is interesting is that the four-cylinder 250 is almost 50lb lighter than the CE and in every dimension is a very small bike indeed. The heart of the bike is an overhead-camshaft engine which looks something like a miniature 500 Honda unit and is, in fact, of basically the same design. Maximum power is produced at 10,500rpm but the engine is safe to over 11,000 where it makes a sound like a noisy sewing machine. If the engine is not revved to its full potential, the fuel economy is excellent and far better than anything possible with an engine of two-stroke design.

Apart from the engine, most other parts of the bike are of conventional design with a front disc, rear drum and standard oil fork dampers and swinging arm. The designers have, however, made the small Benelli appear as modern as possible with a one-piece tank/seat/rear fairing unit. Set in a panel in the front of the tank unit is the instrument nacelle with a tachometer and speedometer. Unfortunately, however neat it looks, the dials are hard to see and take ones attention away from the road. To finish the modern appearance there are cast-alloy three-spoke wheels which look a little odd but are strong and easy to clean. As with the CE, a Moto Guzzi version of this bike is available, called the 254. Its styling is a little different but again is merely badge engineering.

The company did experiment with a bike powered by two of the little 'fours' mounted together to make a 500 V8, but the costs were prohibitive, while a 125cc 'four' developed at the same time as the 250 was thought to be just too extravagant.

3   BENELLI 500

The most striking thing about the 500 Benelli is that it bears more than a passing resemblance to another four-stroke, four-cylinder half-litre machine, the 500 Honda. The similarity centres on the engine which not only looks like the Japanese bike's unit, but also sports the same cylinder dimensions: 56 × 50.6mm. However, with a 10.2:1 compression ratio, the Benelli produces slightly more power with 55bhp available at 9800rpm. The single-overhead-camshaft engine, which is fed by four Dell'Orto carburettors, can push the 440lb bike to a top speed of 112mph. Because of the bike's relatively low weight, fuel consumption is good and 50mpg is easily possible. Although initially available with two powerful drum brakes, the 500 is now equipped with a two disc front and single disc rear layout, a move dictated by the public's reaction to the many disc-braked Japanese bikes. Styling is typically Italian with wide flat handlebars and boxy panels, tank and instruments.

Incidentally, the bike's engine is manufactured at the Moto Guzzi factory in Mandello del Lario, as are all the Benelli four-stroke engines, while the two-stroke units of the two companies are built at Benelli's Pesaro works. This has been the case since motor magnate Alejandro de Tomaso bought out the ailing companies a few years ago. Since that time, the single-cam Honda lookalike engine has been the basis for most of the companies' four-stroke range.

4   BENELLI 750 Sei

When the 750 Benelli was announced it caused no small sensation, for it sported no less than six cylinders. Mounted across the frame, the engine is an impressive sight, although it must be admitted that such a layout has its problems. For example, if the bike had straight tracts for the inlet manifolds, the carburettors would stick into the riders knees. So, the pipes for the three Dell'Orto carburettors are mounted on twisted pipes which bend in under the tank. The other problems encountered with such a layout are the large frontal area offered to the wind and that the bike is very wide and thus difficult to wield in and out of traffic. Apart from those detractions, everything else about the Sei's engine is excellent. The natural balance afforded by such a layout means that the engine is very smooth and the fact that, because the power take off from the crankshaft is at its middle, there is no chance of crankshaft whip as is sometimes possible with other automotive engines of the same configuration.

The Sei is not a highly tuned machine but nevertheless produces 71bhp at 8900rpm and there is a wide and flat torque band which makes high-speed cruising an easy affair. The top speed of the 485lb machine is 115mph and fuel consumption usually stays on the good side of 40mpg.

The Sei has a very sturdy frame and so handling is as good as one would expect for a thoroughbred Italian machine. One criticism was levelled at the machine when it appeared and that was that it was not as powerful as had been expected. One European distributor for the marque produced a 900cc version, while the company itself tried a few twin-overhead-camshaft prototypes. In the end, Benelli exhibited their own 900 in early 1978 which would put Benelli back in the ever-growing race for bigger and more powerful motor cycles.

5 BMW R45

From being in a desperate financial position in the late 1950s, BMW have now turned the tide in the opposite direction and are now enjoying a large share of the top-range-bike market. The success of the company was built around large touring models of 500cc or over and it was not until the middle of 1978 that a new range appeared, the R45 and R65 series, which replaced the larger and older 500 and 600cc models. Much neater and smaller than its predecessors, the R45 nevertheless still weighs a hefty 425lb, the same as its larger stablemate. Two stages of tune are offered on the R45's oversquare engine, 26bhp for the German market, where it gets into a lower insurance bracket, and 35bhp for the rest of the world. On the export version, peak power is reached at 7250rpm, while maximum torque is 27.5lb ft attained at 5500rpm. As is now legendary with these Berlin-built bikes, the engine is of flat-twin configuration with valves operated by pushrods and rockers. It may not be the most modern layout available on a motor cycle but, over many years, it has been improved and developed so that it is reliable, efficient and very smooth. Performance is not a strong point of the R45 but it will reach a top speed of just on 95mph. Fuel consumption on the other hand is excellent, with an average figure of 55 to 60mpg being possible. The bike has a 4.8 gallon fuel tank, so it is obvious that it was made with touring in mind.

Transmission is by five-speed gearbox and shaft drive, while braking is by a single cross-drilled disc at the front and a powerful drum at the rear. Standard fittings on the bike include cast-alloy wheels, audible warnings for the indicators, twin mirrors, electric starter and a plug for fitting an intercom device. The standard of finish is about as good as can be found on a motor cycle, but there is a price to pay for that: the price itself, for the smallest BMW produced is more expensive than many 750s on the market.

6   BMW R80/7

BMWs have never been competitive with machines of similar capacity in recent years, because straight-line performance has not been of prime importance to the company nor it would seem to the riders of its bikes. However, BMW thought it would not be right to be left a long way behind in power, so they replaced their R75 750 with the R80 which actually displaces 785cc. Going a little way up the capacity scale means that tractability and economy are not lost in the quest for extra acceleration and top speed as would happen if a smaller engine had been uprated.

Displacing 785cc, the flat-twin engine produces 55bhp at 7000rpm, which gives the bike a top speed of 115mph. Drive is via a car-type single-plate dry clutch, five-speed gearbox and shaft drive and, although BMW have done a lot to remedy it, the transmission suffers a lot from a clunking effect as gears are changed. The change itself is smooth but it is very positive and slow due to the inertia in the system. Great care has to be taken on slippery roads when changing down as the rear wheel can break traction momentarily, for a shaft layout is not as forgiving as a chain. That apart, the middleweight BMW is safe and predictable in all weathers, a fact which is helped by a powerful cross-drilled disc on the front wheel.

A feature of all BMWs is the long travel of the suspension which makes for a very comfortable ride over all surfaces and this, along with good tyres, keeps the whole smooth and running in a straight line, even over white lines and ridges which would keep other machines weaving. Extra equipment for the bike is available, including large custom-built panniers for the rear which hold as much luggage as many a two-seater sports car, and either of the fairings for the larger bikes from the company, the dolphin 'S' type or full 'RS' type.

7　BIMOTA SB2

Bimota is a company which was formed by messrs BIanchi, MOrri and TAmburini, and is situated in the Italian Adriatic resort of Rimini. They supplied the frames for the Harley-Davidsons with which Walter Villa secured 250 and 350cc World Championships several times and the frame for his only serious rival, the Yamaha of Johnny Cecotto, a combination which won the 1975 350 title. Since then the company have decided to build roadster frames too, and their results are among the most efficient sculptures of metal ever to grace the engine of a motor cycle.

The SB2 is their second design (Suzuki Bimota 2), the first being for a Kawasaki, the KB1 (Kawasaki Bimota 1). The Suzuki design will take either the 750 or 1000cc GS straight-four engine in standard or modified form, although the weight saving over a standard frame is a performance boost in itself. Under the bike's bodywork is a mass of bright-red large-diameter tubing which cocoons the engine, itself a stressed part of the whole set-up. Unlike a normal frame which features a loop cradle and a roughly horizontal top tube, the Bimota has a sharply angled design with the top tubes running from the steering head almost down to the level of the rear suspension pivot. There is no need for a high mounting point for the rear suspension as the Bimota is an intriguing monoshock design.

Strong the massive frame may be, but it would seem at first glance to be a nightmare for any major power unit maintenance. That is where the Bimota's famous split frame comes in. Right in the middle of the top tubes on either side are conical couplings fastened by three socket bolts. Undo these and the frame can be taken away from the engine in around 20 minutes. The secret is that the coupling is male to female so perfect alignment and rigidity is assured.

An hour glass shaped (narrow in the middle to allow for narrower pegs and so more ground clearance) box-section swinging arm is attached to an unusually small vertically mounted spring/damper unit of car design at the bottom of the sloping top tubes. The arm widens around the back of the transmission to pivot exactly where the secondary drive gear emerges, so that suspension movement does not alter chain tension and so give the rear wheel fluctuating torque outputs. It is a simple idea, but something quite rare on a chain drive bike. Front fork design is novel, too, with the fork angle different to the rake of the steering axis, so that trail is kept more constant under suspension travel than is normal.

Clothing the bike is superbly contoured and quickly detachable glassfibre bodywork, comprising a nose fairing, under fairing and an elaborate tank/seat/rear fairing moulding which hold an alloy 3.5 gallon fuel tank and a suede cushion. In all, the bike looks very futuristic, and this accentuated by the standard red, black and white colour scheme. A weight of 21lb for the standard frame helps give the bike an overall weight of just 433lb, which is a saving of around 70lb on the standard GS Suzuki.

The Kawasaki version is different in that it does not have or need the split frame design, it has a normal horizontally mounted monoshock spring/damper rear suspension and is clothed in smoother bodywork virtually identical to the 1977–78 OW-31 and OW-35 racing Yamahas as used by Agostini, Baker, Cecotto and Roberts.

8   BMW R100RS

When the BMW R100RS was announced in September 1976, it was seen as one of the most innovative motor cycles in recent years. Underneath, it was little more than a larger-engined successor to the R90S 900cc bike, but what was different from any other machine was the large fairing. It was clear that there was a great deal more to the bike's bodywork than just appearance and, in fact, there was, for BMW spent a great deal of time in the wind tunnel of the Italian automotive design studio of Pininfarina perfecting the shape.

The fairing increases the frontal area of the machine by quite a large amount which does have a detrimental effect on top speed and performance at high speeds, but there is the advantage that, with the rider's head bobbed down behind the screen, a great deal of weather protection is afforded. One problem with fairings usually is that stability at high speed is sometimes suspect, but this is remedied with the BMW by a lip around the centre of the body which increases downthrust. Incidentally, the lip is in roughly the same position as the downthrust tabs on the faired Moto Guzzi V1000, so obviously the two manufacturers who have had wind-tunnel facilities have come up with the same and right answer.

With the larger engine, now of 980cc, performance is more than adequate with a top speed of just over 121mph. However, one unfortunate BMW trait is exaggerated with such a large engine and that is the bike's tendency to tip to the right if the throttle is blipped at standstill due to the torque reaction of the longitudinal-mounted-crankshaft engine. In fact, the bike is decidedly lumpy at low speeds and much more at home when running at higher revolutions.

Since the R100RS has been in production, the rear drum brake has given way to a cross-drilled disc to match the two at the front, alloy wheels are fitted as standard and a proper dual seat is standard equipment rather than the rear-faired single which was neither a true racing saddle nor proper twin. As is now famous with BMWs, the switchgear is excellent as are the instruments, including the quartz clock which adequately sums up the company's attention to detail.

9 COSSACK DNIEPER MT-9

The Cossack Dnieper side-car outfit is a very rugged and reliable machine, and that has a lot to do with its being an old design. The origins of the bike are a little unclear but it seems as though plans for BMW machines got into Russian hands after the war and subsequently found their way to the Cossack factory, albeit some time afterwards.

Today, the outfit is obviously outdated but to someone who wants a practical form of transport and who is willing to put up with having something which is totally non-sporting in character, the Cossack works. The bike's power unit is the venerable pushrod flat twin which, in this guise, displaces 650cc and produces 32bhp at 5200rpm. Running with a low 7:1 compression ratio means that the

1. BENELLI. The two-stroke Benelli 250 which had all the performance of a Japanese bike with the handling qualities and price of an Italian thoroughbred.

2. BENELLI. Sister to the two-stroke quarter-litre Benelli is the extravagant and wildly expensive four-cylinder 250/4.

3. BENELLI. The Quattro is an unashamed copy of the Honda 500.

4. BENELLI. The six-cylinder Sei was the pioneer 'six' bike.

5. BMW. The R45 is the first of a new generation of smaller and neater BMWs.

6. BMW. The middleweight BMWs, like the R80/7, are popular for touring.

7. **BIMOTA.** Undoubtedly, the SB2 Bimota Suzuki is the best café racer around.

8. BMW. The R100RS was the pioneer of the aero-dynamcally designed fairing for large roadsters.

9. COSSACK. The Dnieper MT-9 sidecar outfit offers cheap transport for three people.

10. **CZ.** The 250 CZ does not have a great performance, but is cheap, reliable and safe.

11. **DKW.** The DKW/Hercules W2000 was a brave but expensive attempt at enticing the public to the revolutionary Wankel.

12.   DUCATI. The 500 parallel-twin configuration Desmo.

13.   DUCATI. The desmodromic-valve superbike from Bologna is the updated 900SS, complete with massive 40mm carburettors.

14.   DUCATI desmodromic-valve superbike engine.

15. FANTIC. The lightweight Fantic with their Chopper 125.

16. HARLEY-DAVIDSON. A 75th Anniversary 1200cc Electra Glide.

17. Harley-Davidson 1200cc engine.

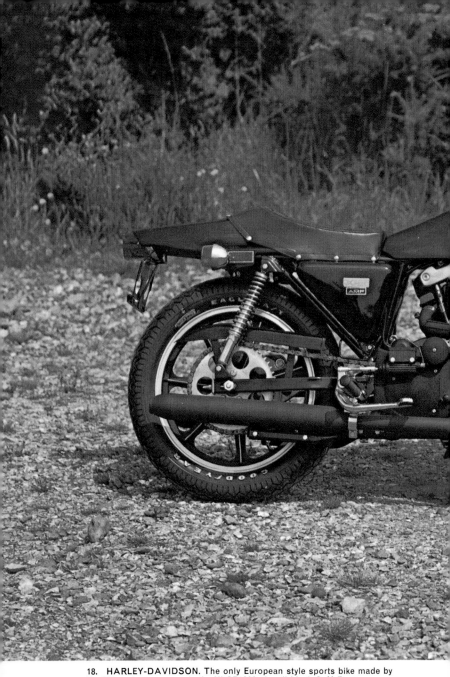

18. HARLEY-DAVIDSON. The only European style sports bike made by the Milwaukee company is the XLCR1000, the all-black Café Racer.

19. HONDA. The CB250N is now designated the 'Super Dream' after the apathetical response to the Americanised styling of its 'Dream' predecessor.

20. **HONDA.** The powerful little 125 twin from Honda.

21. **HONDA.** The single-cylinder XL250S.

22. **HONDA.** The 400 Auto Honda stays as a Dream for the time being.

23. **HONDA.** The much mourned four-cylinder 400.

24. **HONDA.** The 750 was one of the first Honda superbikes and the F2 was the culmination of its development.

25. **HONDA.** Everything about the popular CX500 is unconventional.

26. Honda **CBX** 6-cylinder engine.

27. HONDA. Sporting more than 100 bhp, the CBX is shatteringly quick in a straight line with a top speed approaching 140 mph.

28. HONDA. The GL1000 Gold Wing Honda is a very refined motorbike.

29. INDIAN. This ME-125 is an attractive and well finished machine.

30. KAWASAKI. The KH125 is surprisingly sporty.

31. KAWASAKI. The KH250 was one of the last three-cylinder strokes from Kawasaki.

32. KAWASAKI. The 400cc class is quite popular these days and the Kawasaki version follows the classic four-stroke parallel-twin layout.

33. KAWASAKI. The Z1R is the sports version of the famous Z1000 which held the Kawasaki title of 'King', being the fastest bike of its time.

34.   KAWASAKI. The Custom 650 is easy to ride fast.

35.   KAWASAKI. The Z750 is a Japanese version of a typical British design.

36. LAVERDA. The 175 uses a Zündapp power unit.

37. LAVERDA. The 2TR multi-purpose off-roader.

38. LAVERDA. The Jota is still the sportiest machine built by the Braganze Company, but is only legal in Britain, largely due to its throaty exhaust.

39. LAVERDA. The 500S Alpino is a well bred sports machine.

40. LAVERDA. The 1200 Mirage is almost a 'Jotarised' 1200.

41. **MORINI.** A competitive bike in the Italian half-litre category.

42. **MOTO MERIDEN.** The Co-Uno 125.

43. MORINI. The 3½ Morini is available in single or twin seat form, the Sport and Strada.

44. MOTO GUZZI. The 850 Le Mans is now available with a Spada-style fairing and bodywork.

45. MOTO GUZZI. The V50 is just like a scaled-down 850 in appearance.

46. MOTO GUZZI. The automatic V1000 Convert.

47. MV AGUSTA. The 350S manages nicely as a twin-cylinder.

48. MV AGUSTA. The single-cylinder 125.

49. MV AGUSTA. The Monza developed from the 750 America.

50.	MZ. The East German MZ has a very respectable turn of speed.

51.	NORTON. The famous Commando.

52. **QUASAR.** The Reliant-engined Quasar is like nothing else in motor cycling.

53. RICKMAN. The Rickman brothers keep their hand in with some excellent café racer and touring chassis to take either Honda or Kawasaki power units.

54. ROYAL ENFIELD. Although the name is dead in Britain, the Royal Enfield lives on as a 350 manufactured in Madras, India.

55. SEELEY. Colin Seeley builds bikes like the Rickman brothers, but his are exclusively Honda powered and have very short wheelbases.

56. SUZUKI. The TS185 is the middle range machine in the off-road class built by the Company.

57. **SILK.** Although the British bike industry as a major part of the economy no longer exists, small Companies still thrive. Silk have a long waiting list for their two-stroke 700S.

58.   SUZUKI. The X7 has revived for Suzuki the glories they captured with their 1960s version of the 100mph 250cc bike.

59.   SUZUKI. The GS400 is a dual purpose (sports and commuter) middleweight roadster.

60.   SUZUKI. The GS550 Suzuki gives superbike performance.

61. SUZUKI. The bike on which Barry Sheene's 750 triple racer was based, the GT750. This bike's accent was on touring.

62. SUZUKI. The RE5 was Suzuki's attempt at manufacturing a popular Wankel-engined bike.

63.　Suzuki RE5 Wankel engine.

64. SUZUKI. The GS1000 can handle and corner as well as a lightweight.

65. TRIUMPH. The Triumph range carries on with electronic ignition and revised switchgear. The single-carb version is the Tiger.

66.   TRIUMPH. A British bike with a famous name is the twin-carb version
of the Tiger, the Bonneville.

67.   Triumph 500cc single-cylinder engine.

68. **YAMAHA.** The Yamaha RD250 has a reputation for quick acceleration and fine handling.

69. **YAMAHA.** The DT250 is fitted with monoshock rear suspension.

70.   YAMAHA. The SR500 is a single-cylinder sports roadster that typifies the big British 'thumper'.

71.   Yamaha 500cc single-cylinder engine.

72.   YAMAHA. The XS400 is a four-stroke machine in
the popular 400 class.

73.   YAMAHA. The XS500 is a parallel-twin four-stroke machine.

74. YAMAHA. The XS1100 is an XS750 with an extra cylinder and a 'bit more capacity'. It is blisteringly quick in a straight line.

cheapest grade of fuel can be used and that fuel consumption will be good. A figure of over 56 miles per gallon can be achieved which is good for a 650 and excellent for an outfit of any kind. The penalty one pays for this is the performance, for a little over 60mph is all that can be reached in the top ratio of the four-speed box; incidentally, the Dnieper in side-car form also has the luxury of a reverse gear which comes in handy as the combination weighs just under 700lb and is too heavy to push out of kerbs, for example.

Apart from the inherent handling difficulties side-cars present, the Cossack has one other fault and that is that it comes with the bike mounted on the left of the chair, the opposite to normal practice.

Seating is available for three people with one in the chair and one each on the single rubber saddles of the bike, the pillion unit being mounted on top of the rear mudguard with a grab handle bolted on to the seat base. The Cossack can be made into a complete touring outfit for the options available make it a very well equipped machine. There are leg guards for the rider, a stereo for the chair and a trailer which can be hitched on the back which can also take a tent unit.

10   CZ 250

Although the Czechoslovakian Jawa and CZ companies are separate entities, they are both state owned and geared together to help each other rather than take each others' potential markets. In fact, just about all the main parts of the Jawas, apart from frame and electrics are made at the CZ works. The CZ 250 is very near the top of that company's range, with only a motocross-type Enduro more expensive and powerful.

The basis of this Eastern bloc 250 is a twin-cylinder, two-stroke engine which, although not a high-speed unit, nevertheless produces a respectable 17.5bhp at 5250rpm. This gives it a top speed of just on 70mph, while standing start quarter mile acceleration takes 19.5 secs; fuel consumption is not exceptional as it consumes petroil mixture at the rate of 50mpg. Unlike some other small CZs and the Jawa 350 (which is very much a stretched 250

CZ), the bike does not have the companies' Posilube or Oilmaster automatic lubrication which, these days, is something of a sad omission.

Power from the engine drives through a four-speed gearbox which is the most unusual and ingenious feature of the CZ. Firstly, the left-foot gear-change pedal is pressed in towards the crankcase and swung back where it acts as a kickstart. After the motor fires up, the pedal is put back into its original position where it acts like the slick-shift units fitted to Triumph bikes a few years back. To change gear, the hand clutch is not needed, for slight pressure on the gear pedal releases the drive so that a new ratio can be chosen. In operation, it needs a positive yet smooth foot to control it, but after practice it is even possible to select first gear while stationary and pull away.

Where the CZ loses out to the opposition is in the braking, for the drum unit at the front is rather spongy in operation and not too effective, while the pedal for the rear is too far away from the footpeg. The handling of the 350lb bike, on the other hand, is excellent and trouble free, although the tyres do not grip too well in the wet.

Just like most from the Eastern European countries, it is well equipped with a rear-view mirror and large toolkit, including hand-pump, as standard.

11 DKW WANKEL 2000

Due to a British bicycle factory's having the rights to the name, the motor cycles of Nurnberger Hercules Werke AG are sold as DKWs in Great Britain. The company's most interesting bike is the Wankel 2000, which was the first ever motor cycle to feature the rotary engine designed by Dr Felix Wankel. The 2000's power unit is a derivative of a snowmobile engine manufactured by proprietary unit builders Fitchel & Sachs, and differs from it by the adoption of an electric starter to replace the rewinding pull cord of the winter sports device. The single-rotor unit is cradled underneath the frame and mounted longitudinally, although the rotor itself sits across the bike which makes for interesting gyroscopic effects when cornering.

After driving through a six-speed gearbox, the power has to be 'turned' for the chain drive, although this was not a problem with the prototypes as they were housed in shaft-drive BMW frames. However, with 32bhp and 24.5lb ft of torque at hand, the bike had to make do with something smaller than a large BMW type chassis. All together, the production 2000s weigh 350lb, so performance from the 294cc engine is brisk, with a 100mph top speed possible. The capacity of a Wankel is a very interesting point, with varying views on whether it should be classed according to the capacity of one, two or three chambers of three-lobed rotor. Unfortunately, it seems that most people regard the bike as being of 588cc, twice the stated amount, while the bike has the performance of a good 300 and the fuel consumption of a 900, at around 34mpg. This is not praising the Wankel at all but it must be remembered that the engine is in its infancy of development and that cars built by NSU in the 1960s were not very fast or frugal machines. However, automotive engineers seem to have overcome that obstacle on four wheels now, and it remains to be seen whether the same can be done for bikes. In operation, the Wankel 2000 two-stroke is noisy and not as smooth as one would expect, but its ability to rev freely and quickly gives it an urgency that is unmatched by reciprocating piston engines.

After substituting the petroil system for direct injection and adding other refinements to the bike, Hercules decided to drop the Wankel as it was not competitive on a cost/performance basis with conventional bikes, but given time and money that could be rectified.

12 DUCATI 500 SPORT DESMO

The Ducati 500 Sport Desmo is one of the new breed of increasingly popular half-litre sporting bikes which most of the important manufacturers are now making. This 500 is a 180° parallel-twin four-stroke which like the Darmah and 900SS features desmo-dromic valve operation. The practicality of such a system is debatable on road bikes for, although the mechanical opening and closing of the valves means that valve bounce is eliminated, something has to be done to modify the rest of the engine before it is able to rev to limits where conventional engines would run out of breath. Further, some form of spring is usually advisable to make sure that the valve is shut when starting and such a system is very difficult to design and worse to keep running satisfactorily, with service intervals measured in hundreds instead of thousands of miles. However, the layout works well enough in the Ducati and, even if the company is shy about disclosing power outputs, the bike is well able to match its rivals, with a top speed of over 110mph and the ability to cover a quarter mile from start in 13.5 secs. Fuel consumption is only barely as good as its larger stablemates at 45–50mpg so with a 2.6gal tank fuel stops have to be very frequent on long runs.

The Desmo is a very nimble bike on the open road and the rear set pedals and clip-on style bars make sports style riding easy and enjoyable. With three disc brakes to take care of just on 400lb of bike, stopping is easy and fuss free in all weathers with no premature locking or fade. The fact that the 500 is aimed at the rider who enjoys riding fast is accentuated by the saddle being large enough for one person and a very close friend and no more; also, rear foot pegs are not a standard fitting. Were a passenger accommodated, the rider would find that sitting forward would make things very uncomfortable with the controls.

Switchgear and instruments, although adequate are not of the same quality as larger Ducatis, but Italian bike enthusiasts are used to that.

Although the middleweight Ducati has been available for only a few years, it is likely to be replaced by a small version of the famous Taglioni vee-twin which will give an even greater impression that the 500 Desmo Sport is a Darmah shrunk in the wash.

13/14   DUCATI DARMAH

The Ducati Darmah is in all respects a thoroughbred motor cycle in the best tradition of the great Italian manufacturers. Named after a fictional tiger, the Darmah does have something of a tiger quality with its effortless power and agility. The power unit of the bike is a 90° vee-twin engine mounted longitudinally in the frame with the rear cylinder offset to the right of the front. Like the other large Ducatis, it has a capacity of 863.9cc but only the 900SS shares the same desmodromic valve system, as designed by famous race-engine builder Fabio Taglioni. Although not as well endowed with horsepower as some Japanese bikes, the 65–70bhp put out by the engine has to power considerably less weight than the competitors, so performance is not that far behind. Top speed is just on 115mph, while a standing start quarter mile takes just over 13secs. As with all big Ducatis, fuel consumption is excellent, being between 45–50mpg most of the time. Where the bike does score over opponents is in the handling and road-holding sector of perform-ance for, with light weight, good balance and a sturdy frame, this bike is just about *the* quickest on a twisty road. Like Vincent, Ducati use the engine as an integral part of the frame with the front downtubes bolting on to the bottom of the crankcase, having the cylinders one behind the other makes the bike narrow so that the handling and roadholding can be exploited to the full. Other now almost standard Italian chassis parts include Brembo discs all round, Ceriani forks at the front and good-looking but expensive Campagnolo wheels.

Ducatis have never been the most attractive bikes (except in an engineer's eyes, perhaps), but with Leo Tartarini taking a hand in styling, they have gained a new image. The Darmah features neat tank and tail bodywork which, with subtle striping, look neat and racy. Also, Nippon Denso instruments have been put on to replace the suspect items of older models and an electric starter is there to save the aggravation of kicking the plot into life.

The Darmah is the touring version of the famous 900SS which has a 9.5:1 instead of 9.4:1 compression ratio and the option of 40mm instead of 32mm carburettors. With a dolphin fairing less weight by virtue of a manual starter and more power (80bhp is claimed), the 900SS is an unashamed road racer and top of the Ducati range.

15 FANTIC CHOPPER 125

The word chopper when connected with motor cycles conjures up visions of outlaw gangs of bikers with their Triumph and Honda-powered custom bikes, but to the Italian Fantic company it means a neat 125cc bike on sale to the general public. Their Chopper comes with a 125cc Minarelli engine which is hardly enough for a bike gang to terrorise a neighbourhood, but enough to make an unusual-looking lightweight a spirited performer.

The lower half of the bike's frame is fairly conventional, but the duplex cradle rises up at the front way past the engine to the steering head where it meets the long outstretched front forks which angle away from the bike one way and join on to large 'high-rise' handlebars the other. To go with the image is a thin 16in tyre at the front and a large almost car-type 5in wide × 16in cover at the rear which, with just 15bhp to transmit to the road, should last a long while. In spite of the bike's unaerodynamic appearance, performance is good with a top speed of 70mph possible; fuel consumption is good, too, with the bike using approximately one gallon of petroil mix per sixty miles. However, as the bike uses a 'peanut' tank of just over a gallon capacity, fuel stops should be frequent. Behind the 'peanut' tank is the 'king and queen' seat (another spin-off from outlaw jargon) which is surprisingly comfortable, although the low-slung rider squab will present problems for those riders who are over six feet tall. The pillion is altogether better catered for, with a higher seat and a large comfortable back rest. On the rear of the rest as well as in between the handlebars there is lattice work bracing which makes the bike just a little bit too gimmicky.

Handling the bike is not the nightmare one would expect a chopper to be and, in fact, once used to the somewhat awkward riding position with the footrests almost in front of the engine and the downward pointing bars, cornering is brisk and trouble free. Although only sporting small drum brakes front and rear, stopping is no problem as the bike weighs a mere 230lb.

What the little Fantic does best, of course, is attract a great deal of attention and not many bikes, let alone 125s, do that. If you live in Italy and want the looks, but less power, the company also does a 50cc version, which must make it the ultimate moped.

The Electra Glide Harley-Davidson is probably the most famous motor cycle ever, and certainly the machine that made Milwaukee famous is the one bike which just about anyone in the street can identify readily.

For 1978, the familiar 45° vee-twin engine of the Glide was uprated from its famous 1200cc to a full 80cubic inches, which is 1338.8cc, making it the largest capacity bike ever built by the American company and one of the largest built by anyone anywhere.

With 722lb of weight to carry, the Glide needs all the power it can get and is still only just able to reach the magic 100mph in its latest guise. Just to save the Glide owner from any nightmares, a centre stand is not fitted, and the bike has to be rolled on to its massive crash bars for any repairs or wheel changes. The company boasts that the bike has the widest tyres available for its flagship and they really do grip the road in the dry, even to the point of screeching when they start to break traction. In the wet, however, the beast deserves the upmost respect for they are quite willing to break away even at low speed. The single disc units mounted at either end are not nearly as effective as the drum units of older models, and this is one point where Harley-Davidson would have done better sticking to their famous traditions.

The rider tucked behind the large fairing has a beautifully contoured fully sprung seat to sit on which easily compensates for any harshness in the suspension, while there are neat foot boards instead of the usual pegs. The footboards are necessary as trying to pivot one's right foot on to the car-like rear brake pedal would be impossible if you tried to keep the ball of your foot in touch with the bike. Just to emphasise the car-like style of the Glide, a foot-operated clutch pedal is available to special order; this would rule out even further any pretentions one might have to sports riding. The Electra Glide is purely a tourer, though, and the makers even believe that the rider will have plenty of time to look down at the tank-mounted speedometer and operate the tank-mounted light switch, such is the lazy style of the machine. Mounted as standard at the rear is a large top box and colour matched side panniers, each with its own chrome-plated crash bars.

On the road, most 250cc machines will romp away from it from a standstill but there is no better machine made for travelling two-up with as much luggage as you would want in supreme comfort over as many continents as you would have time for.

18 HARLEY-DAVIDSON XLCR1000

Aside from the Aermacchi manufactured two-stroke lightweight motor cycles of the early 1970s, the Café Racer Harley-Davidson is one of the more unique variations of the famous American concern. What the bike is and what it appears to be (a road-going lookalike of the company's XR-750 road racer), may not be that much alike, but the Café Racer name tag is an admission that this Harley really wins the most points in the cosmetic stakes. Underneath the looks, however, is a powerful and manageable sports bike which, although only as sophisticated as the other ancient vee-twins in the range, competes favourably with many other machines of later ancestry. As enthusiasts would say, the Harley-Davidson *is* the engine, and the Café Racer uses a high-compression version of the redoubtable overhead-valve narrow-angle vertical vee-twin, which has very undersquare dimensions of 81mm × 96.8mm, giving a capacity of 997.5cc. Maximum power of the bike is 68bhp at 6200rpm while the torque is, to quote the manufacturers, at 3500rpm more than any other machine available. Top speed of the Café Racer is limited by its low gearing, for it rushes up to the red-line speed of 106mph with apparent ease. The sprint like quality of performance is accentuated by its 13secs dead time for the quarter mile. A five-speed gearbox would raise the top-end performance, but just as with the venerable vee-twin, a four-ratio unit is part of the company's tradition.

With a long wheelbase and large grippy tyres on alloy rims, the Harley corners and handles well, and this is helped by its deceptively low weight of 485lb. The performance of the twin Kelsey Hayes discs at the front and single unit at the rear are, however, not up to the task of stopping the beast adequately, while wet conditions will make them barely noticeable at all.

The Café Racer's most distinctive feature is its colour which is black virtually all over, something which might make safety conscious environmentalists shudder, but which to an enthusiast is mouth watering. The screen of the small fairing is dark-grey tinted, the wheels are black, 90% of the engine is black; and even the contorted snake-like siamese exhausts are black; it would probably be wise of the rider to wear a dayglo orange suit to compensate. One bad design of this and all Harley-Davidsons is the indicator system which consists of push buttons on either side of the bars. The indicators operate only while the button is depressed which, to say the least, is hazardous when trying at the same time to operate the main controls.

19   HONDA CB250N

When the CB400F2 four-cylinder was decided to be unsuitable for the American market, and therefore the world, Honda had to produce a twin-cylinder bike with at least as much performance, and came up with the Dream, or Hawk as it was known in the USA. It was also decided that a smaller version could be made for the quarter-litre class and this would also help make their four-stroke 250 quicker and more in keeping in touch with the opposition's quicker two-stroke machinery.

Thus, the 250 Dream was introduced but, after the Europeans said that the styling was too American, it was dropped in favour of the 'N' series, better known as the Super Dreams. At that time, Honda hoped they had finally got their mix right!

The engine of the 250 is a four-stroke air-cooled twin which features three valves per cylinder, two inlet and single exhaust driven from the single overhead camshaft. They allow better breathing and therefore more performance and economy. To keep the engine smooth, the motor has the now almost universal contra-rotating balance shafts. Power output of the engine is 27bhp at 10,000rpm, just a couple of horsepower down on the admittedly lighter 'strokers'. This power is fed through a six-speed gearbox and performance is to the order of a 90mph top speed and 16.5 secs standing start quarter mile time. Fuel consumption is 65mpg.

The CB250N weighs around 350lb so is quite heavy, but this does not affect the handling unduly, and the bike remains well balanced and easy to ride. The wheels on the bike are the famous Comstars which unlike the earlier Dreams which had alloy rims and pressed-steel spokes are now all alloy and a lot lighter.

The styling is the most obvious change of the Super Dream and it has a simulated one-piece tank/seat/tail unit to replace the earlier bike's more touring look. The modern sports look of the replacement model is probably overdone with its tank stripe a rich colour by the saddle only to fade out as the paintwork reaches the steering head and the computer-age-digit numerology on the side panels.

20   HONDA CB125T

While the competition finds it more economical and easier to build their lightweight motor cycles with two-stroke power units, Honda has persisted with motors of four-stroke design to the detriment of weight and performance. Honda had two 125s in production: a pushrod single with an amazing economy, the CG125, and a sports version with an overhead camshaft engine, disc brake and more performance, the CB125J (which, incidentally sported a CB125S badge on the side panel).

However, even the J model was not quick enough to rival other manufacturer's wares, so Honda decided to build a completely different bike in the same class, and so came up with the twin-cylinder, overhead camshaft CB125T. The bike's engine features just oversquare dimensions of 44×41mm, displacing 124cc, and breathes through two quite large 22mm carburettors. With its compression ratio of 9.4:1, the engine produces 16.5bhp at 11,500rpm, while the red line is just on 12,000rpm. Performance is brisk with a top speed of 75mph, while fuel consumption is good, too, averaging out at 75mpg. Not surprisingly, the engine's torque output is not great at low engine speed, and the motor has to be kept spinning above 7000rpm before it pushes the bike's 251lb weight with verve. For more performance, a six-speed gearbox would be better than the five-ratio unit fitted.

The CB125T has a single down tube frame which bolts to the engine making it a stressed member, while steel pressings are used for the other attachment to the steering head. Braking is by a cable-operated disc at the front and drum at the rear.

The Honda is a comfortable machine, and with a seat height of 30ins (as tall as many larger bikes) it should suit tall riders who find many lightweights difficult to ride. The pillion rider is well catered for, too, with the rear footrests mounted on the frame and not like so many small bikes on the swinging arm, where the passenger's legs go up and down with the road undulations.

Honda have paid a lot of attention to styling recently and the CB125T is a particularly attractive model with its one-piece-look tank and side panels, grab handle at the rear and stylish upswept twin exhaust pipes.

21 HONDA XL250S

Honda's XL250 trail bike was at one time rather outclassed by its competitors as it was a great deal heavier and not nearly as potent. However, the XL250S is a much better machine with a lot less weight and an innovative new engine.

The power unit of the 250 is an all-alloy single-overhead-camshaft single which features four valves, making its breathing easy and efficient. Power from the oversquare unit peaks at 20.2bhp at 8500rpm which gives the bike a top speed of almost 80mph, yet a fuel consumption which is decidedly frugal at 70mpg; on the road, of course. An interesting feature of the engine is its exhaust system which features twin pipes, claimed by the manufacturers to be superior to a larger-bore single unit for low-speed torque. Power is fed via a wet-multi-plate clutch and five-speed gearbox to the 18in rear wheel, which looks rather odd considering that the front is a massive 23in diameter. However, as has been found in motocross, larger front wheels make things a lot easier on really tough ground. The performance of the XL off the road is excellent and the bike is a lot more than just a trail/fun bike for it could well be a competitive club racer.

Many trail bikes are hard to ride on tarmac purely because their knobbly tyres just don't grip. However, the Honda uses Yokohama covers which are of specially developed dual purpose type and so make road work a little less of a nightmare experience. In fact, with such light weight (260lb), the off road Honda makes many pukka roadsters seem clumsy.

The bike is liberally scattered with good ideas like an engine decompressor which works automatically when the kickstart is used, which takes all the strain out of that. There is a neat instrument cluster which houses the speedometer with a place set on the side for milometer and reset trip meter, which makes things just about ideal for the enduro competitor.

All in all, the XL250S should suit anyone interested in doing anything off road, except perhaps GP motocrossing, for the bike is a superb performer, and a smooth one at that. For this machine has a single-cylinder engine with a balance shaft to cancel out vibrations at high revs, which makes it one of the most well engineered bikes available.

22   HONDA CB400 AUTO

Automatic transmissions may seem somewhat unnecessary on motor cycles, but they are very popular in the United States and, as theirs is such a large market, it dictates that more should be made. The Honda 400 Auto is unique in that it is the first of the new-generation autos as a middleweight roadster rather than superbike, like the 1000cc Convert Guzzi and 750 Hondamatic.

The 400 is the CB400 Dream and, like the manual version, is a four-stroke, twin-cylinder machine. The Auto's engine differs in tune from the manual and has 30bhp at 8000rpm compared to 43bhp at 9500rpm. Torque is down just a little to 20.25lb ft at 6000,which is 2000rpm lower down the rev range than its sister bike and much more useful for its semi-automatic gearbox which has just two gears. The modifications are by way of smaller carburettors, smaller ports and milder camshaft. The three-valves-per-cylinder (two inlet, one exhaust) twin with chain-driven contra-rotating balance shafts in auto guise is a very smooth and well-mannered machine indeed, even if performance is not a strong point.

The bike's gearbox is not truly automatic in the car sense, being a two speed unit with torque converter and manual change. First gear is for up to 50mph, while second will take the machine to its top speed of 95mph.

Riding the 400 requires a new technique. The bike will only start if the gear selector is in neutral and the gearchange order is neutral at the bottom, with the two gears 'up', second above first. Should you forget to take the bike out of gear and put the side stand down, a failsafe switch will cut-out the ignition, thus preventing the bike from taking off without the rider.

The bike works remarkably well if just left in the higher of its two ratios and will pull away, albeit fairly slowly, from second gear. As can be expected, even using both gears, acceleration is not startling, with a standing start quarter mile time of 17.2 secs. Fuel consumption is good, however, and can average out at just on 60mpg.

With the exception of the gear-position indicator replacing the unnecessary tachometer, and a parking brake replacing the clutch lever, the CB400 Auto is just like the pre-Super Dream manual version with its 'Americanised' styling and attractive Comstar wheels.

23   HONDA CB400F2

The 750 Honda four-cylinder, which appeared in 1969, was the first in a vast range of fours from the giant Japanese company. Although most were upwards of 500cc, one model was marketed using an engine of 350cc mounted in a chassis that gave it an appearance similar to that of the 360 twin. More successful than that early 'small-four' venture, however, was the CB400 which was granted Super Sport nomenclature by the company. Like its larger stablemates, the 400's power unit is an across-the-frame, single-overhead-camshaft, four-stroke engine which, in its later modified F2 guise, produces 37bhp at 8500rpm. In fact, breathing through four Keihin carburettors, the engine will rev freely right up to its 10,000rpm red line with no fuss, and a formula one car like shriek replacing the usual smooth clock like whirr of the motor. The power is transmitted through a six-speed gearbox which may seem rather extravagant, but which in reality is very necessary, for the bike thrives on revs and is not that powerful lower down the engine speed scale. For instance, if the bike is cruising at 70–75mph in sixth gear and the rider runs into a strong headwind or starts to climb a motorway hill, the bike will lose pace fairly easily, thus necessitating a change of gear. This is even more pronounced when riding with a pillion aboard.

However, if the engine is kept spinning at a high rate, the 400 is turned into a very quick machine with a top speed of 103mph and a standing start quarter mile time of 15secs dead. With such an efficient little engine, fuel consumption is excellent with over 50mpg being attainable under most conditions.

The frame of the 400 is an interesting design with a single downtube running from the steering head through the centre exhausts where it is split into a cradle that winds round under the crankcase. It looks and is very sturdy and gives the bike very taut handling qualities. This is helped by the fact that all the considerable 395lb weight is kept low. Smaller riders will find that the little machine is very easy to handle in traffic and to put on and off the centre stand.

Unlike most other Japanese bikes, the CB400F2 has not been overburdened with unnecessary braking and retains just a single disc at the front and a drum at the rear; the front disc has a neat cover incidentally which keeps out a great deal of water in the wet.

Unfortunately, Honda decided to stop production of the 400 four, as the buyers in the large American market really wanted easy-to-maintain twins. The European market thought that this would be a retrogressive step, so the fours were snapped up from dealers in the hope that they would be collectors items when the twin Dream series arrived. However, sources in 1978 suggested that a completely new range of small fours would be built along with the twins, using twin-overhead-camshaft engines and ranging right down to 250cc.

24   HONDA 750F2

The 750 Honda was arguably the first of the new range of superbikes when it was announced in 1969, and even the rival, the earlier-announced Triumph Trident, had one less cylinder than the Japanese bike's four. Steadily, the Honda was developed from its initial K1 guise until in 1978 it was available in K7 form. During that time, what was the incredible performance of the early bike had dissolved, as the power unit was modified to suit pollution regulations. In a bid to resurrect the performance to meet the ever-growing competition, a Super Sport F1 version was announced, which featured sportier looks, if not a lot else. The F2 was an altogether different proposition, however, with a completely revised engine which was hoped to keep customers happy until Honda's sixteen-valve twin-cam range was ready.

The F2's engine is a 736cc single-overhead-camshaft four which, with larger inlet and exhaust valves than the F1, produces 6bhp more at 73bhp at 9000rpm; torque peaks at 46lb ft at 7500rpm. Although not as sophisticated as other Japanese fours, the Honda unit is nevertheless powerful and very smooth and able to give the bike a top speed of just over 120mph. Cosmetically, the F2 is far removed from its predecessors and its looks bear more than a hint of the famous Honda Formula One racers. The matt-black engine has an air of quality about it as do the steel Comstar wheels. The original Honda 750 was the first mass-produced bike to be fitted with a disc brake as standard, and since that time every manufacturer has adopted them. This sporting Honda has three: twin front and single rear, with floating calipers and slotted brake pads.

Handling has never been the 750's best point, but the F2 is an improvement over the rest with its revised suspension. The Japanese tyres are not as safe as European covers, however, on this particular bike.

The standard of finish on Hondas is high, and the F2 is no exception, with the chrome on the four-into-one exhaust, which finishes at the tail of the bike with a width of no less than five inches, standing out in particular. Night time riding on the F2 should be easy with a powerful quartz halogen headlamp cutting a path.

More like the endurance racers is a limited edition F2 which features a 'Phil Read' twin headlamp endurance style fairing, finished in Honda Great Britain colours. That, until the sixteen-valve series comes along, should keep the road racers happy.

25 HONDA CX500

Honda's offering in the increasingly popular half-litre class is unlike any of its competitors, and unlike any other Honda before, being a water-cooled vee-twin, with a longitudinally seated crankshaft.

Unlike most other vees, the CX500 has its cylinders mounted at an odd 80° with the cylinders then twisted by 22° so that the mixture goes straight from the hidden carburettors into the combustion chamber and out of the exhaust without any power-consuming twists. Having that set-up also means that the carburettors are conveniently out of the way of the rider's legs. Of course, the main problem with the twist of the cylinders is that it rules out the possibility of employing overhead camshafts, so the CX has instead a central cam operating lengthy pushrods. These, in turn, operate rockers on either head which are connected to the four valves per cylinder. Not only does the engine rev freely with such efficient breathing, but it is also powerful, producing a maximum 50bhp at 9000rpm with its 10:1 compression ratio.

The engineers at Honda thought that air-cooling would not be efficient enough to dissipate so much engine-generated head, so a liquid-cooled system was built on to the bike. This has the added bonus of making the bike a lot quieter than it would normally be.

The CX500 has a contra-rotating clutch which helps negate the inherent torque twist which pulls the bike to one side, and it transmits the power through a five-speed gearbox to a shaft final drive. The engine and transmission unit hangs from a stiff spine frame and, although it is rigid and helps the handling, it does add even more weight to an already heavy machine which, in all, tips the scales at 450lb. With this bike, Honda decided to keep a drum rear brake, along with twin front discs, just to make sure that the bike can be stopped adequately whatever the weather. In reality, they are well able to stop the machine from its top speed of 108mph. Not only is the CX500 technically different from all other bikes, but it looks different, too, with its wide saddle, large black radiator and odd casing around the instruments which looks rather like a small nose fairing with the screen removed.

Considering that Honda had a 500cc four-cylinder machine at one time, the CX500 may seem a backward step, but underneath is an advanced technology which makes the middleweight bike one of the most interesting available.

26/27   HONDA CBX

Honda were the last of the Japanese manufacturers to build a sports 1000cc bike, although they already had a one-litre machine with the touring-style Gold Wing. Instead of tuning that bike, they decided to build a roadster on the lines of their endurance racers, of straight engine configuration, with twin camshafts and four valves per cylinder. Two models were tried: one a four-cylinder not unlike their CB750 machine and the other a six-cylinder model. In testing the six was found to have around 5bhp more than the smaller version and it was thought that this along with the obvious sales charm of a bike with more cylinders would be enough to keep the customers satisfied. 1978 saw the arrival of the Honda CBX which was received with mixed blessings: some thought it was fantastic, while others saw it as the superbike war escalated out of all proportion.

A lot has been done to try to keep the across-the-frame straight-six narrow and co-designer Masahuri Tsuboi managed to keep the crankcase from being little broader than the Honda fours; above that, the cylinders are obviously wider. The engine is very much an oversquare unit with dimensions of 64.5×53.4mm, giving a capacity of 1047cc. Six Keihin carburettors are mounted in a broad vee fashion so as not to obstruct the riders knees and help give the engine a maximum power output of 105bhp at 9000rpm, maximum torque of 62.2lb ft at 8000rpm and a red-line figure of 9500rpm. Top speed of the 548lb bike, with its large frontal area to penetrate the wind, is 140mph, while it will accelerate over a quarter mile from a standing start in a little over 11.5secs. Fuel consumption is around 35mpg, depending on how hard the bike is used.

There seems to be something odd about the bike when first seen and it seems hard to say just what, that is until it is realised that there are no down tubes on the frame. In fact, the engine hangs from a large spine structure, with the wheel thus closer to the engine and so offering a shorter wheelbase for better handling. In fact, that is handy for the bike would have been even more ponderous in its road manners had the wheelbase been longer. Quite safe on smooth roads, the CBX can be tricky when the going gets rough. Three disc brakes (twin 11in units at the front and a 12in at the rear), mounted on Comstar wheels, cope surprisingly well with stopping the big bike from high speeds. Like the CX500, tubeless tyres are fitted.

With a curious mixture of styling curves and angles, the CBX may not be to everyone's taste, but one glimpse at the remarkable engine would bring to mind that oft-quoted phrase 'racing improves the breed'.

The four-cylinder prototype later saw the light of day as the 900cc CBFZ.

28   HONDA GOLD WING

The Honda GL1000 K2 Gold Wing, built to rival the BMW and Moto Guzzis, is the flagship of the Japanese giant's touring fleet. This bike, more than any other, has a great deal of motor car technology built into it and that accounts for its weight which, at 584lb, is in the super heavyweight class. The heart of the machine is a flat-four (or Boxer) configuration engine of 999cc set low in the frame; this feeds through four carburettors to the valves which are actuated by a single rubber-belt-driven camshaft for each cylinder bank. With water jacketing around the cylinders, the size of the unit is accentuated even more.

Drive is via a five-speed gearbox and shaft, another example of car technology. Chain drive on such a heavy and powerful machine would need adjustment every one hundred and fifty miles or so and on a long-distance tourer like the Wing that could mean stopping during a journey to carry out the task. Honda decided to adopt the shaft-drive principle at the expense of the inherent clunking gearchange of such a system.

Although smooth and extremely quiet, the bike's engine produces no less than 80bhp which gives the Gold Wing a more than respectable performance with a top speed of 123mph and the ability to cover a quarter mile from rest in 13.2secs. Fuel consumption can be heavy if the bike is pressed too hard, but with normal use petrol will be consumed at the rate of approximately 35–40mpg.

The big Honda is quite deceptive in appearance, for the fuel tank is under the seat and not above the engine where it appears to be. In fact, the 'tank' is a dummy which has a cover which lifts to reveal a neat little oddments tray; also inside are catches which open panels on either side of the 'tank'. The left reveals all the electrics, while the right houses a lever, which acts as a kickstarter when inserted in the engine, and the header tank for the radiator, which is housed behind the front wheel. Having the fuel tank under the seat helps lower the centre of gravity which enhances the handling which, in itself, is good rather than great. However, the Honda Gold Wing is a tourer and never happier than with a large fairing and panniers, making it the nearest thing to a two-wheeled car . . . albeit with a true motor cycle performance.

29 INDIAN ME-125

Indian is a name from the history of motor cycling which is synonymous with large touring motor cycles like Harley-Davidson, some of which were of four-cylinder configuration.

More recently, the Indian name and, indeed, the famous logo, have appeared on completely different motor cycles from a company based in Beverly Hills, California. In fact, since the demise of the great company, there have been many attempts to revive the name, although the present one is the only one which seems to have succeeded.

The present Indian company markets a range of small roadster and trail machines, the most potent of which, although not the largest, is the ME-125. The little 125 trail bike is quite a mixture for, although the Indian headquarters are on the West Coast of America, the bikes themselves are manufactured in Taiwan with engines from the proprietary unit firm of Minarelli in Italy.

The bike's engine is a conventionally ported two-stroke single of 123.48cc which produces 16bhp at 7200rpm and drive is via a five-speed gearbox. What alters the performance of the engine on this Minarelli-powered bike is the exhaust system, two-strokes being very sensitive to exhaust design. The elaborate plumbing of the

Indian seems efficient, though, as it produces 1bhp more than the similarly equipped Fantic and 2bhp more than the Barron. Top speed of the bike is just on 75mph, while it will return upwards of 60mpg. The ME-125 is very much a dual-purpose vehicle for, while it has a lot of ground clearance and the off-road norm of 17in rear and 19in front wheels, the rest of the machine is aimed at the commuter-type motor cyclist, with mirror, indicators and a rear carrier as standard, something very few roadster manufacturers think of.

Performance on the rough is something of a compromise, too, for not only are the tyres not that grippy, but the whole bike is not really sturdy enough for the enthusiastic mud-plugger who enjoys leaping bikes and generally 'giving his bike stick'. As a part-time trail machine, the Indian is useful and fun, however.

One small criticism is the exhaust, though. Efficient it may be and attractive it certainly is as it sweeps out, round and over the engine but, even with a guard, it gets terribly hot and tends to make the rider sit bow-legged when the machine is still in traffic.

30   KAWASAKI KH125

With many companies turning their attentions away from two-stroke bikes, because of their pollution problems, it was surprising to see Kawasaki pursue them with a small range of commuter 'strokers'.

The KH125 is typical of the line being a tiny but very nippy motor cycle. The heart of the bike is its single-cylinder engine which is canted forwards in the frame. The oversquare unit uses a disc valve which makes it more powerful, economical and cleaner than normal piston-ported units, and this is exemplified in its power output which is 14.5bhp produced at 7500rpm; this is combined with a torque output of 10.5lb ft. Top speed in the highest of its six gears is 72mph, while standing start quarter mile acceleration takes 18.2secs. Obviously, the bike's miniscule weight of just over 209lb is a contributing factor here. Fuel consumption of the self-mixing variety is around 70mpg which is not far away from that of the slower four-stroke machines in the same category.

Braking is taken care of by a disc at the front and drum at the rear which are easily up to the task. The front disc is one of the very few on the market which is cable operated, but on such a small bike it is hardly noticeable.

Although not intended as such, the KH125 is rather sporty in appearance and this is further accentuated on the bike as the rider leans forward quite a lot to the bars, making the whole plot look like a mini racer. This does not mean that it is uncomfortable, however, and even two up you will find that long trips are well within the bounds of possibility before you start aching. The KH125 is well equipped with a fuel tank that will give the lightweight bike a range of over 170 miles, a neat tool compartment in the rear fairing and a mirror. Earlier bikes had mirrors either side, but the manufacturers later thought that the second one was unnecessary.

31 KAWASAKI KH250

The KH250 Kawasaki is an air-cooled two-stroke three-cylinder bike, the only triple in its capacity class and, like its larger sister machine the KH400, the last of a famous breed of fast strokers from the Kawasaki Heavy Industries Group. In the late 1960s and early '70s, Kawasaki's triples had a reputation for being difficult to handle, very dirty (with their two-stroke smoke following at all times), uneconomical and very very fast; so fast, indeed, that the larger models could be somersaulted backwards from a standing start with little difficulty. With environmentalists forcing manufacturers to build cleaner and more frugal machines, Kawasakis lost a lot of their famous edge in performance until by the late 1970s they were docile and very maneagable machines indeed.

The KH250 has its three cylinders set across the frame which displace 249cc and, with a compression ratio of 7.5:1, produces 28bhp at 7500rpm and 19.5lb ft of torque at 7000rpm. Top speed of the machine is around 95mph, while it will cover a standing start quarter mile in 16secs. The performance is accompanied by a high-pitched whine which is more in keeping with a bike of half its size. If all the performance is used, the KH250 can still be a very thirsty machine and return less than 30mpg. However, if treated with restraint, a figure of well over 40mpg should be possible. Although the KH250 still emits a great deal of smoke under hard acceleration, oil consumption is quite comparable to many seemingly cleaner machines.

The Kawasaki frames have never had the best of reputations, but that of the KH250 copes remarkably well, the bike not having an excessive amount of power (unlike its predecessors) helping this no end. A single disc brake is fitted at the front while a drum is mounted at the rear.

As is typical with Kawasakis, the instruments and switchgear are excellent and a nice touch is the handlebar-mounted choke lever which is a boon, as the little bike is sensitive to it on cold mornings and would present problems fiddling around for the device by the carburettors.

Unlike its competitors, Kawasaki do not have comparable four-stroke machines in their range, but that time cannot be far off, because although the KH250 and the much faster KH400 are among the most exciting machines in their classes, there will be no place for them in the conservation-minded 1980s.

32 KAWASAKI Z400

The Kawasaki Z400 is an air-cooled four-stroke twin, like most of its competitors and, by its specification, a touring/commuter machine rather than a sports bike. However, again like its competitors, it does have a fair turn of speed and is not quite the bland machine that the '400' tag implies.

Although just a twin cylinder, the Kawasaki is a smooth and well developed bike with its balancer-shaft 360° engine. Valve actuation is by a single camshaft mounted overhead, while breathing is via two Keihin carburettors. The engine is red lined at 9000rpm, while maximum power is developed at 8500 (35.7bhp) and maximum torque (23.7lb ft) at 7000rpm. This means that to extract the most performance, the engine has to be revved quite hard, but as the unit is well balanced and smooth, it doesn't make things too tiresome. The engine is coupled to a six-speed gearbox with the ratios well spaced. The top speed is 102mph which is just on the red line and, as the maximum speed in fifth is a fraction over 90mph, the top ratio could be a bit longer for more relaxed high-speed cruising.

Fuel consumption is one of the Z400's stronger points and it can average over 55mpg, while being able to cover over 85mpg if the speed is kept down. The fuel tank holds 3.1gals which should enable a touring range of over 180 miles.

The middleweight Kawasaki has quite high bars which make it extremely comfortable around town, although they do make high-speed travel tiresome after a while. As 75–80mph is the bike's limit before it sounds fussed and stressed, this should not be too much of a problem.

The bike uses a broad duplex frame with conventional springing which is well able to cope with the demands of the average rider. The same can be said for the tyres which, with a softer compound than the notorious covers used some time ago by the Japanese industry, work well in all weather conditions. Braking by a single disc at the front and a drum rear is adequate rather than exceptional.

The Z400 perhaps gets forgotten among the famous machines from the same stable and its less than sporty image does not help it at all, but as a practical and well engineered bike with a surprisingly good performance, the Kawasaki does its job well.

33 KAWASAKI Z1R

In the late 1960s, Kawasaki was planning to produce a 750cc version of its four-cylinder 650W, but were taken aback when Honda beat them to it with their CB750. Instead of putting their twin-cam 750 on to the market straight away, they waited and developed their bike into a 1000cc monster which would not only be bigger and faster than the opposition but also lay the ghost of the frighteningly rapid H1 500 which took the world by storm in 1968. The prototype 1000s which were sent for evaluation to America returned with the summing up which nobody at Kawasaki expected: they were too quick. So, the final design for the export market was based around a mere 903cc unit. After emission controls took their toll of performance, the full 1015cc unit was put on the market several years after the 'King's' introduction. The 750 version was marketed in Japan, however, where larger machines were prohibited.

A yet later version of the 1000 is the Z1R which has a revised engine, different body panels and a neat fairing. This bike is intended as a stop gap until Kawasaki's six-cylinder range is ready.

The famous Z1000 engine is a four-cylinder four-stroke twin-overhead-camshaft unit which uses four carburettors and roller bearings for the big ends. All in all, the unit is remarkably smooth and produces its power in a turbine-like manner. The Z1R has 7bhp more than the standard Z1000, which puts the figure at an amazing 90bhp produced at 8000rpm. The bike's top speed is 131mph, while it will rocket through the quarter mile in just 12.1secs from a standing start. When all the performance is used, fuel consumption is very high and the rider, if he has time, can watch the fuel gauge, which sits next to a matching ammeter, go down.

At high speed, the little fairing comes into its own and does divert the wind away from the face and body, even though it does look no more than a cosmetic item.

The brakes on the Z1R are three cross-drilled discs which are meant not only to save weight but also get rid of water in the wet, thus making them more efficient. In reality, however, they work no better than the usual stainless-steel discs and that is not a compliment. The bike, at 542lb, is quite heavy and the brakes need to be gripped strongly in the dry, too. Even though the Z1R is one of the fastest bikes available, the American market has a quicker version which utilises a turbocharger. Not surprisingly, with around 25% more power, the Turbo Z1R is not so much a quick bike but more a road-going drag racer.

34 KAWASAKI Z650

The middleweight Z650 Kawasaki looks a lot like its larger stablemate, the Z1000, but they are quite different and just share the same appearance and basic specification.

The heart of the bike is a four-stroke twin-overhead-camshaft four-cylinder engine which, with four carburettors, produces 64bhp at 8500rpm and 42lb ft of torque at 7000rpm. With the bike weighing 465lb, this gives a top speed of 121mph and enables it to cover a quarter mile from a standing start in 13.3secs. Unlike the bigger bike's power unit, the Z650 uses plain main bearings but they detract nothing from the smoothness of the unit which is one of the quietest around. However, when accelerating hard, the normal purr is turned into a roar at the end of the four-into-two exhaust system. As the engine is so efficient, fuel consumption can be very good at lower speeds, with 45mpg on the lowest grade of fuel being possible. A 3.7 gallon fuel tank should ensure that the rider does not have to stop too often on a long journey.

The bike's handling although not as vicious as the early 900s can be worrying if the rider corners near the limit of the tyres, for the bike will tend to wallow when power is applied. That is only when the bike is travelling at speeds which would be foolhardy most of the time on public roads, however. Braking is by a single disc at the front, while a drum unit is utilised for the rear, but they are not up to stopping the bike repeatedly from high speed as they tend to fade quickly.

Like Yamaha who build a 650cc twin, Kawasaki resurrected that particular engine size and gave it, in their case, an advanced multi-cylinder engine which, in outright performance, is inferior to the Z1000 but nevertheless in a smaller bike makes for an adequate road burner. To quell thoughts that the bike's main failing was dated looks, Kawasaki introduced two other versions, one, the SR, for America only, had high-rise handlebars and a dual-height seat, along with minor engine modifications, while the other is the Custom with alloy wheels, three disc brakes and minor styling changes: in all, a good-looking and very fast middleweight machine.

35 KAWAŞAKI Z750

Fitting neatly in between the Z650 and Z1000 four-cylinder bikes in the Kawasaki range is the Z750 which is a parallel twin with a touring rather than sporting image.

What Kawasaki have done is take the much-loved formula of

vertical-twin and added to it the technology of a modern age, complete with twin camshafts, balance shafts, anti-pollution devices and all.

The four-stroke Z750 has an engine of square dimensions of 78mm which gives a total capacity of 745cc and, breathing through two Mikuni carburettors and on an 8.5:1 compression ratio, the power output peaks at 55bhp at 7000rpm. Outright power at the top end of the rev scale does not make full use of the bike, however, as it pulls strongly from low revs thus putting an accent on to fast touring rather than sprinting. Unlike the other big twins on motor cycling history, the Z750 does not vibrate a great deal, this being achieved with contra-rotating swing weights which oppose the primary forces. Another point which demonstrates the technology put into the bike is the fact that it has crankcase ventilation which recycles gases back through the carburettors, thus reducing hydrocarbon emissions. Of course, the twin overhead camshafts are also part of the specification usually set aside for sports multi-cylinder machines.

Power is fed through a gear primary drive to a five-speed gearbox which, in turn, drives a conventional chain to the disc braked back wheel; there is a single disc at the front, also.

Early Kawasakis were not renowned for their handling qualities, but the 481lb Z750 with its sturdy duplex frame copes remarkably well, even though it is not in the 'road-scratching' class; the high touring bars are no help when the rider tries hard, either.

Unlike Yamaha and Suzuki who were the first to develop self-cancelling indicators, Kawasaki on the Z750 use the ordinary audible system which bleeps in time with the flash of the warning light. What Kawasaki did introduce, however, is a neat safety device which cuts off the starter circuit when the clutch is engaged. This means the lever has to be pulled in before the engine can be fired.

36   LAVERDA 175

Zündapp of Munich produce a range of small two-stroke machines themselves, while for some time they have also marketed their engine/transmissions separately for other manufacturers to use. When Laverda decided to market some small two-stroke bikes themselves they decided that it would be easier to buy the proprietary German units rather than spend a great deal of money developing their own. When the 125 and 175 Laverdas were announced, they were seen as typical of the company's products, whether caravans, farm equipment or bikes: expensive but brilliantly engineered and immaculately finished with a modern style unique to them.

The Zündapp engine is a 163cc single which features water cooling for better efficiency and quieter running but, unlike larger machines which require water pumps, this unit relies on the thermosyphon system whereby hot water from the jacketing rises into the radiator while the cooled liquid there follows that elementary law of physics and goes down to the engine again: simple but effective. Because the engine is small and doesn't produce that much heat, a fan is not needed, either.

The oversquare engine (62×54mm) produces 17bhp at 7000rpm which gives the bike a top speed of 75mph, while fuel consumption is around 70mpg. The performance is not spectacular for a 175 and many 125s are not far off that in top speed, but the extra capacity does make things a little easier and less fussy, while the engine's smooth and quiet operation means that the Laverda can be cruised at high speed without the tiresome nature of a smaller air-cooled unit. A five-speed gearbox is fitted on the bike.

The rest of the machine reads like a who's who of expensive and high-class parts manufacturers. The electrical system is Bosch, suspension by Marzzochi, brakes by Brembo (disc at the front and rod-operated drum at the rear), tyres by Dunlop, while the wheels are alloy units from Campagnolo, some of the most expensive made.

The frame, of course, is Laverda's own and is simple yet sturdy which makes handling virtually viceless.

As can be imagined, the 175 Laverda is an expensive bike, and costs more than most 400s and almost as much as some 500s, but Laverda compete with other bikes on paper and specification rather than on price, and they have never found that a problem.

37   LAVERDA 2TR

Laverda of Breganze, a small town in the shadow of the Dolomites in northern Italy, is famous for its large roadster bikes, but over the past few years it has produced several off-road machines, from competition 125 and 250cc motocros and enduros, to the all-purpose 250cc 2TR, a bike which is basically for trail riding but which can also be used for small trial or enduro events. Laverda have collaborated with the Swedish Husqvarna concern on many matters and use their engines on competition machines. The 2TR, however, has a Laverda power unit which was designed by the Husqvarna team, being a simple piston-ported two-stroke single.

With square 68 × 68mm dimensions and a 10:1 compression ratio, the 247cc motor produces 30bhp at 7000rpm, a figure which is better than most road-going twins. Due to its off-road gearing, the Laverda has a lower top speed than a roadster style machine, but at 75mph it should be enough for a machine using knobbly tyres. Acceleration away from rest is very rapid and it is quite easy getting the front wheel airborne. Fuel consumption depends a great deal on conditions and terrain, but 40mpg is quite possible if mostly ridden on tarmac.

The 2TR is the most adaptable off-roader made and this is due to its easily adjustable steering geometry. The forks are pivotted at the top and there is a bolt which secures the unit in one of three positions. Basically, they are with the fork near vertical for trials riding; in the intermediate position for general off-road work or enduro; or angled forwards for easier road riding.

Another important feature which should ensure minimal maintenance is the enclosed rear chain which keeps it out of the harmful way of dirt and stones.

The Laverda is more rugged in appearance than many trail machines, and it has none of the appendages that might get in the way and hinder performance, the one exception being a neat little carrier mounted on top of the tank which has a window for a map: very useful if proper trail riding is undertaken.

A version of the bike better equipped for road use with twin instruments and chrome mudguards is manufactured and designated the 2T.

38 LAVERDA JOTA

Jota is the name of a Spanish dance which is in triple time, and is also the name of the 1000cc three-cylinder sports bike in the Laverda company's range. The bike was developed using factory endurance racer parts and was finished off at the British importers with more efficient exhausts than standard, but which were also very noisy and illegal in most European countries.

The bike's engine is an air-cooled four-stroke three-cylinder unit of 980cc which with a 10:1 compression ratio produces 90bhp at 7250rpm. Breathing of the engine is by three carburettors and twin overhead camshafts, while drive is through a five-speed gearbox (with right-foot change). Top speed of the bike is just on 140mph, while it will accelerate to a quarter mile from a standing start in a little over 12secs; fuel consumption will average out at around 40mpg. The performance of the bike is quite different from other large bikes and is not at all turbine smooth or silky. It is, in fact, rather brutal and, like the rest of the bike, not the sort of thing for the faint hearted.

The gearbox casing is massive and more what one would expect to see on combine harvesters made by the same company, and the gearchange is hard and imprecise at low speeds with neutral just about impossible to select at rest. The bike's frame is a large duplex unit which gives the 475lb bike sure-footed handling, while cast-iron Brembo discs on the cast-alloy wheels make the braking just about as good as is possible.

The Jota is a very large bike and quite a handful for riders under 5ft 10in, and the absence of a side stand does not bolster the confidence of the smaller person. However, that apart, the Laverda should suit everyone for the riding position is completely adjustable. The clutch and brake lever can be adjusted for reach, the bars themselves can be adjusted for height (either almost flat, or the more popular racing position) and the gear pedal can be re-positioned on its splines to suit.

One aspect where the Jota's performance is not up to the rest of the bike is in the electrics. The starter motor does not always have the power to turn the engine over, especially after a run with the headlight on, for the alternator just doesn't produce enough. Bump starting is difficult, too, with such a high compression engine.

In all, the Jota is a powerful bike, but it does need a powerful rider who can overcome the heavy clutch, gearbox and heavy low-speed handling.

39   LAVERDA 500

The Laverda 500S Alpino is an updated version of the older plain 500 which at one time had the name Alpina, although this is also the name of a company marketing performance parts for BMW cars and so could have been confusing. The main difference between the two bikes is in the engine, where the later version has a balance weight geared from the end of the crankshaft.

The engine of the 500 is a 180° twin of air-cooled four-stroke design and features four valves per cylinder operated by twin overhead camshafts, driven from the centre of the crankshaft. In an attempt to minimise vibrations, the S model has a bob weight gear driven from the left hand side of the crankshaft and turning in an opposite direction to the crank itself. In reality, it makes the new bike a little smoother than the old one but it is not that noticeable. The S also has a higher compression ratio which gives it a little more horsepower and torque, but since the new bike Laverda have stopped quoting power figures. The older 500 had 44bhp at 10,300rpm and approximately 33lb ft of torque, which is excellent for a half-litre machine, and the revised version has around 4bhp more with roughly the same torque output.

Top speed of the S is 111mph, while it takes exactly 14secs to cover a quarter mile from a standing start. Fuel consumption is approximately 42mpg. The Laverda is fitted with a six-speed gearbox, the ratios of which are very close together, but it would probably get by just as well with a five-gear unit. Unlike the larger bikes from the factory, the 500 has the gear pedal on the more conventional left side.

The bike has a single down-tube frame which is siamesed at the bottom of the crankcase to cradle the engine, and is of sturdy design to make the handling of the 375lb bike predictable and fuss free; Pirelli tyres help roadholding, too.

Laverda use cast alloy wheels made in their own foundry for the 500 and the larger bikes in the range, and in this case are fitted with twin discs at the front and a single at the rear, all of cast iron and manufactured by Brembo. They are a lot easier to handle in wet weather than stainless steel items, and they give the bike excellent stopping power. Prototype 500s were fitted with a one-piece tail/rear mudguard the same colour as the tank and front mudguard, but the 500S has separate chrome units, all of a high standard and not the shoddy and easily rusting items at one time associated with bikes of the Italian industry.

A 350 version of the 500 is available for the Italian home market where it is in a cheaper tax bracket.

40   LAVERDA MIRAGE

Laverda with their Jota had at one time the fastest motor cycle in production but with the arrival of the 1000 Suzuki, 1100 Yamaha and CBX Honda, this was put in some doubt. To combat this, the Italian company produced the Mirage, an uprated version of their 1200 which itself was an update of the Jota but intended for touring rather than high-speed 'scratching'. The Jota-style 1200 is quite similar to all the other machines in the upper end of the Laverda range, thus sharing the unusual three-cylinder engine.

The Mirage is a four-stroke triple with its pistons mounted on a 180° crankshaft with the outer two at top dead centre while the centre one is at bottom dead centre. The more usual arrangement is the 120° layout à la Triumph Trident. In effect, the Mirage has a four-cylinder engine with one cylinder lopped off so that it misses one beat every three firings. Laverda claim that this arrangement breaks up the rhythms which cause high frequency vibration, but instead it makes the big bike sound and feel quite unlike any other.

The Mirage uses the same 8:1 compression of the 1200, the modifications being Jota type high-rise and larger overlap camshafts and more efficient but noisier silencers. Laverda do not quote figures for the bike, but it should have approximately 90bhp and an abundant supply of torque, enough to give a top speed approaching 140mph and plenty of acceleration. Again like all the other triples, the Mirage features an oil-cooler to help keep the engine temperature down.

Where the Mirage does differ from its stablemates is in the suspension, although the same robust double loop frame is still used. The bigger bike no longer has the forward rake forks which made the Jota rather heavy to handle at lower speeds and this has further been helped by the adoption of the flatter bars from the 500. The rear dampers are inclined more on the larger model, too, and they give more wheel travel for the same amount of deflection than the more upright 1000 models.

Other differences of the larger bike are a more shapely saddle for increased pillion comfort, a grab rail for said passenger, different fuel tank and the inclusion of a side stand, as standard.

41   MORINI 500

Morini were intending their 3½ to be a full 500 before it was announced but then decided it would be a little less risky and made it a 350 so that it would be more popular because of its lower tax rating. It was not until mid 1978 that a production version of the half litre machine was ready. Like the 3½, the 500 is a vee-twin of 72° configuration and is exactly twice the capacity of the 250 at 478.6cc. Also as with the other Morinis, the 500 uses a Heron-type head: instead of having a combustion chamber in the cylinder head, it is situated in the piston and so the head can be flat and cheaper to produce. Valves in the 500 are at 90° to the piston and drop down into recesses in them. Drive to the valves is from a single centrally mounted camshaft which itself is driven from the crankshaft by a toothed rubber belt. This has the advantage of not needing lubrication and having a much smoother and quieter operation. A compression ratio of 11.2:1 is used which would normally mean harder starting than the already difficult 3½, but the larger bike does have an electric starter, mounted unusually lengthways on the side, so that bevel gearing is needed to transmit its power through 90°.

Primary drive is by helical gear to the multi-plate clutch which is unusual in that it is dry and not, as is often the case, running in an oil bath; a five-speed gearbox is employed. The 500 does not have much more power than the $3\frac{1}{2}$, peaking in fact at 43bhp at 7500 (a DIN figure), but more important is the torque which is just under 32lb ft at its maximum, which is usefully down the rev range at 5100rpm. Maximum speed of the bike, at the red-line of 8200rpm in fifth, is 110mph, while fuel consumption is approximately 52mpg.

Like all Morinis, the 500 is blessed with excellent handling and this is helped by an adjustable steering damper. The bike is perhaps overbraked with the twin discs at the front and single disc rear easily stopping the 367lb bike, and great care has to be taken to stop premature locking. A major disadvantage for a rider used to Japanese bikes is the right-foot gearchange which is not the smoothest available and somewhat awkward in operation.

The 500 comes with cast alloy wheels as standard and a solenoid operated fuel tap which opens when the ignition is switched on.

42 MOTO MERIDEN CO-UNO 125

On the fuel tank of the Co-Uno 125 is the name Moto Guzzi with underneath, the word Meriden, so that it can be read as either the name of the bike's manufacturer or the name of the company that assembles it.

The workers co-operative at Meriden in the West Midlands of England, manufacture Triumph Tigers and Bonnevilles, the famous 750cc twins that have long been the backbone of one of Britain's most famous makes. The Meriden factory is large and could not run by making expensive and high-powered bikes alone, so with not nearly enough capital to build their own lightweight, they got together with automotive magnate of the Italian industry the Argentinian Alejandro de Tomaso to arrange to assemble Moto Guzzi 125s in England (de Tomaso owns the sports car company bearing his name, Maserati, Innocenti, Benelli and Moto Guzzi). This was agreed and production started.

The engine of the Co-Uno 125 is a further complication of matters being built at the Benelli factory on the Adriatic coast of Italy for the sister company of Moto Guzzi at Mandello del Lario in the lake district.

The unit is a simple piston-ported two-stroke which displaces

120.6cc and produces a healthy 15.4bhp at 7800rpm. Fuel, which is mixed in the bike's tank is put into the engine by a 22mm Dell'Orto carburettor.

Maximum speed of the bike is just on 70mph, while fuel consumption is excellent with a figure of 90mpg easily possible.

The engine is mounted in a proper cradle frame which is surprisingly stiff, making the light bike (212lb) a very taut machine indeed. The small Grimeca front disc and drum at the rear are not quite in keeping with that sporting image, however, and are a little suspect under heavy application.

Where the Anglo/Italian bike does take a distinct second place over Japanese rivals is in the electrics, for there is no battery to boost the system which is annoying on a proper motor cycle rather than acceptable for a moped. Although its overall looks are sporty and the bike is well able to stay with the opposition in performance and handling, the finish of the Co-Uno is more akin to a cheap economy model with a tiny speedometer as opposed to the more accepted norm of large twin instruments; no mirror is fitted as standard either.

That detracts, perhaps, from a nimble and sound motor cycle underneath.

43   MORINI 3½

The Morini 3½, so named because it has 'three-and-a-half-hundred' cubic centimetres in its engine, comes in two forms, a touring version called the Strada and the appropriately named Sport.

Both have a 72° vee-twin engine mounted longitudinally in the frame like Ducati, the other famous motor cycle manufacturer in Bologna. The engine is an interesting design for both con-rods work on the one crank throw which means that the offset of the two cylinders is very small and thus makes an inherently narrow engine design even narrower. Plumbing of intake and exhaust on such an engine design presents problems and indeed on the 3½ there is great difficulty when cold starting. The engine has two separate Dell'Orto carburettors and both have choke levers mounted on them which are very difficult to get to. As the engine is very sensitive when cold, the choke is quite critical and it does mean either waiting till the engine is hot before moving off or fiddling under the tank to get the right mixture until normal operating temperature is reached. That aside when the engine is running hot it is a very smooth sweet sounding motor indeed.

Both bikes are of 344cc, while the Strada has a 10:1 compression ratio to the Sport's 11:1. Power outputs are 39 and 42bhp, respectively, although these are SAE figures and not the more popular and accurate DIN ratings. In both forms, the engine is red-lined at 9200rpm and so with 14.4mph per 1000rpm in the highest of the six gears, the $3\frac{1}{2}$s are obviously a little overgeared. However, a tall ratio in top helps the fuel consumption which is around 65mpg, excellent for machines in the sporting 350 class. Top speed is around 100mph for both bikes.

Unlike the 250, the $3\frac{1}{2}$ has 12 volt electrics but does have one rather unique feature. A red warning light is mounted on the control panel which glows all the time the ignition is switched on, while a neutral indicator light would be a much better idea, especially as neutral is especially difficult to find with the bike at rest.

The most obvious differences between the two 350 Morinis is the styling, for the Strada is a two seater with straight handlebars, while the Sport features a neat racing-style saddle and clip-on type units. Both have a single disc brake at the front and attractive alloy wheels.

44   MOTO GUZZI LE MANS

The 850 Le Mans is the sportiest bike produced by Moto Guzzi from their factory by the shores of Lake Lecco in Italy, and has a low and lean look which reminds you of something straight off a race track. However, although the Le Mans is indeed a very quick bike, it is smooth and deep-throated and not like a screaming racer at all.

The bikes power unit is an 844cc 90° vee-twin which runs on a high 10.2:1 compression ratio. It produces 81bhp at 7300rpm and will rev to 8000rpm without harm, but also has an abundant supply of torque over a wide rev range, so it will pull strongly from low speeds even in high gears. Power is transmitted via a car-type single-dry-plate clutch to a five-speed gearbox and thence to a shaft drive. This makes gearchanging rather ponderous and the gears cannot be rushed at all. Top speed of the bike is 135mph, while it will accelerate over a quarter mile from a standing start in 13.5secs. Fuel consumption is an excellent 48mpg.

The 850 Le Mans sports Moto Guzzi's patented integral braking system which is both ingenious and simple. The right-side foot pedal goes to a master cylinder and, through simple valves, distributes 75% of the force to the left-side front disc and 25% to the disc at the back, so giving ideally balanced braking so that one wheel doesn't lock up prematurely. This saves the rider having to work out the required amount of co-ordination himself and is useful on wet roads and in emergencies. A normal brake lever on the handlebar operates the other cross-drilled cast-iron disc at the front and gives a little more retardation. The company says that it is for emergencies or sports riding, but it is more likely to give confidence to the uninitiated rider, for it would be far simpler to have all the brakes worked by the one pedal.

The Le Mans is styled in the manner of café racers with low bars and rear-set pedals. Early bikes had a single seat to give extra rear support for the rider but later models adopted a pillion cushion. However, the passenger will feel rather vulnerable on it as the rider will still be in the same crouched position.

A lot of criticism at one time was levelled at the tiny little nose fairing of the bike, but at high speeds it does indeed deflect the air far enough around the rider to make things more comfortable. Moto Guzzi, it should be remembered, have a massive wind tunnel in which they developed their famous dustbin-fairing-equipped racers so are unlikely to add a 'cosmetic' screen. Early models came with a wide dayglo orange band on the fairing, but this was dropped on later bikes.

45   MOTO GUZZI V50

The 500cc class V50 Moto Guzzi looks like a scaled-down version of the larger roadsters from the same Mandello del Lario company, but apart from all being 90° shaft-drive vee-twins, they are somewhat different. The V50 is a very oversquare unit with dimensions of 74 × 57mm bore and stroke which, with a compression ratio of 10.8:1 make it a high-revving two-valve twin indeed. Unlike the 850 and 1000s, the valves of the pushrod V50 are parallel working in conjunction with semi Heron-head combustion chambers set into the pistons. The 490cc unit produces 45bhp at 7500rpm, although the unit is red-lined at 9000rpm, and has a wide power band which makes for good acceleration, especially with the whole bike having a dry weight of a miniscule 334lb. Top speed is 105mph, while a 14.2secs time is possible for a standing start quarter mile.

The engine drives via a car-type clutch to a five-speed gearbox and then to the shaft driven wheel. The shaft does make gearchanging a little slower and more sensitive to engine revolutions, although this disadvantage is balanced out by not having to bother with chain adjustment and replacement. Braking is by Moto Guzzi's patented integral system where by using the foot pedal 75% of braking is given to the front wheel, while the rear gets the remaining 25%. The difference between the V50 and the larger Guzzis is that it has a very close fitting cover over the rear unit which is to keep it drier in the rain. If this does work and does not hinder the brake from dissipating heat, they could well be used on the front twin units as well.

The V50 is quite a low machine and has a very sturdy frame, with box-section alloy swinging arm at the rear. In true Italian tradition, handling is excellent (helped no doubt by the light weight), while Michelin tyres make roadholding superb, too.

Not like typical Italian machines of yore is the switching and instrumentation which is of high quality, although a combination of red, green, blue and yellow warning lights and switches may seem confusing at first. There is a lockable cover over the fuel filler cap (which gives access to the 3.6gals tank) and, nicely out of harm's and the element's way, the brake fluid reservoir.

A V35 350cc version of the bike is also available and is essentially the same as its larger stablemate, but more suited to Italy's tax laws.

46   MOTO GUZZI V1000 CONVERT

The V1000 Convert Moto Guzzi is probably the ultimate touring machine, for not only is it built in the upright riding position style of the famous Electra Glide Harley-Davidson, but it also has the luxury of a semi-automatic gearbox.

The Convert uses a 949cc version of the famous vee-twin four-stroke engine which was designed for a small car to be used by NATO forces and which then found its way into military bikes and then to the famous V7 Guzzis.

In Convert form, it produces 71bhp at 6500rpm which gives the bike a top speed of 112mph and enables it to accelerate over a quarter mile from standing start in just over 14secs; excellent figures for such a machine. Fuel consumption is good, too, averaging at 43mpg.

Power is transmitted by helical-gear primary drive to a torque converter which has a stall gearing of approximately 3:1 and which locks when 1:1 is reached, so giving variable ratios in between. The Fichtel & Sachs converter then drives two gears which give ratios for either town work (low) or high speed (high), although the combination can be used if full acceleration is needed. A shaft final drive is used, too, like all large Guzzis.

The system differs from that of the Honda in that the Guzzi has no neutral as such, and a normal clutch lever is used for starting. The starting procedure is as follows: switch on, swing up side stand, which acts as a parking brake lever as well as an ignition cut-out, then pull in clutch lever and fire engine. The clutch lever can then be released and just a touch of transmission 'creep' will be experienced. From then on, the bike will drive like a pure automatic. One disadvantage of such a transmission is that there is little or no engine braking effect and, just like cars, the Guzzi's brakes have to be used more than normally. However, the bike has the famous integral Moto Guzzi system, so it is easier and far more efficient than would normally be the case.

Apart from neat tab spoilers on the crash bars ahead of the engine, the Convert shares the same styling as that of the 850 T-3 Californian with a large tinted, adjustable-for-height screen, running boards, 5.3gal tank and pannier cases.

The Moto Guzzi V1000 Convert is slower, thirstier and heavier than a bike with normal transmission, but for the serious tourer it offers many advantages which take the strain out of riding vast distances.

47   MV AGUSTA 350 SPORT

Like most bikes in the range of MV Agusta, the 350S is the most expensive machine of its capacity available, but also like its stablemates, it is fast, stylish and every inch a thoroughbred.

It may come as a surprise but the 350S does not have the multiplicity of cams, valves and gears that MV are renowned for with their racers, but instead is based around an ordinary air-cooled four-stroke twin-cylinder engine which features overhead valves actuated by pushrods and rockers. The unit is of 349cc actual capacity and breathes through two Dell'Orto carburettors, with the mixture being compressed at a ratio of 9.5:1 in the cylinders; power output is 34bhp at 8500rpm, while the engine feels unburstable right up to the 10,000rpm redline. However, the engine vibrates and clatters a great deal, so restricting revs to the level at which maximum power is produced should give a smoother ride and increase the life of the engine. Due to the high compression of the motor, kick-starting can be difficult, and the engine can hold an average side rider at the top of the kicking stroke quite easily. A right-foot operated gear pedal, in the old tradition of British and Italian bikes, is used with an unusual one-up-four-down change pattern; again, this is reminiscent of vintage bikes.

Although the bike does shake and vibrate, it does have a good performance with a top speed of 104mph and the ability to cover a standing start quarter mile in 15.3secs. Fuel consumption is good, too, if a restrained throttle hand is used, and can average out at over 60mpg. With a massive 4.2gal fuel tank, a touring range of over 250 miles can be achieved, which is a lot better than many pukka touring bikes, and nobody can ever mistake the middleweight MV as a tourer.

With an excellent racer-like chassis, the 350 is endowed with remarkable handling and roadholding qualities, and has earned praise as one of the best bikes in this respect in the world.

MV commissioned famed Ital Design car stylist Giorgetto Giugario to design the bodywork of the 350 and, like the Italjet's designer Tartarini's work with Ducati, the result is simple but very attractive with a one-piece tank/seat/tail fairing unit. Although it is just possible to squeeze a pillion aboard, there are no rear pegs so it will be uncomfortable for everyone concerned. To further complement looks, a full dolphin racing-style fairing is available, while on the other hand a touring version with the same mechanical specification can be purchased in Italy. The difference is that the 350GT has flatter bars, a proper dual seat and blue-and-gold paintwork to replace the famous fire-engine red of the 350S.

48   MV AGUSTA 125

Like all machines in the Meccanica Verghera range, the 125 Sport is very expensive for its size, and a quick appraisal of its specification and performance would reveal that on this bike there is not a great deal of sophisticated engineering or luxury extras to warrant its high price tag. If MVs were marketed under another name, they would probably lose a lot of prospective owners, for the name is automatically linked with the famous fire-engine-red racers which have won no less than 37 World Championship road racing titles. On all bikes leaving the factory, there is a sticker on with 37 stars to indicate this.

The little 125 shares a lot of its technology with the bigger 350 in that it has a pushrod engine, in this case a single-cylinder unit of 123.5cc. The motor is light alloy with a cast iron barrel and on a 9.5:1 compression ratio produces 14bhp at 8500rpm. Maximum torque is just over 7.5lb ft at 7000rpm which is not a great deal. Performance, therefore, depends a great deal on the weight of the rider, but the MV should reach a top speed of just over 70mph. Fuel consumption is as one would expect from a small four-stroke, and the 125 can return an overall figure of 84mpg.

A wet-multi-plate clutch is used and a five-speed gearbox is fitted which has the foot pedal situated on the traditionally Italian right-hand side. Braking is by a disc at the front and drum at the rear.

The frame is similar to that of the 350 with a pair of strong tubes running straight from the headstock to the tail of the bike, with a single downtube which bolts to the engine and triangular centre section meeting the rear of the engine by the pivot for the swinging arm. The whole unit is extremely rigid and probably able to handle many times the power of the 125. As it is, it copes easily with the bike's 228lb weight, and handles as well as any machine currently in production.

Other features on the bike are both good and bad for, while, for example, the 125 has electronic ignition, the brake light works only on the rear unit, which is a little out of keeping of what is expected of a modern bike. One neat touch is the seat which, like the 750 series, is suede covered. When the rider wishes to carry a pillion, the tail section can be slid back on those frame tubes to reveal more of the cushion. In standard position, it is a rear rest so that the rider can make full use of the clip-on-style bars and racer-like handling. To complete the image, a full dolphin fairing can be ordered.

49 MV AGUSTA MONZA

MV Agusta have never seriously produced motor cycles at all, in the context that Count Agusta made a living from manufacturing Bell helicopters under licence. It was his hobby to make motor cycles and the fact that his 'fire engine red' machines have won 37 World Championships, far more than anyone else, is just coincidental.

The company has also produced a range of touring and sporting roadsters, the most famous of which have had engines very similar to the four-cylinder four-stroke twin-cam units fitted to the famous racers.

The MV Monza is developed from the double identity (touring/sports) America 750S, and differs in that it is an out and out road-going racer.

The distinguishing aspect of the big MV is the engine which is an awesome sand-cast alloy unit, indeed from the same moulds of the track bikes. The unit differs in that it has only two valves per cylinder, instead of four, but it has the same twin overhead camshafts driven from the centre of the crankshaft by gears, an expensive but very accurate means. Breathing through four 27mm Dell'Orto carburettors and with a compression ratio of 9.5 :1, it can be imagined that the 837.7cc engine is in a high state of tune. Indeed it is for it produces 95bhp at 9500rpm, and is safe right up to 10,000rpm. Ignition is, interestingly, by a car-type distributor. Top speed of the bike is in the region of 140mph, although it is geared for something approaching 160mph. Primary drive is by gear and goes to a wet-multi-plate clutch and thence to a five-speed gearbox and shaft drive. The change is light and positive and suffers none of the slowness associated with many drive shaft layouts.

The power unit sits in a sturdy but low frame which keeps the centre of gravity down and so enhances the excellent handling and roadholding characteristics.

An extravagant and unnecessary part of exclusive Italian bikes is the black suede seat which although gripy and soft stays soggy for days after a shower of rain. Like the smaller 125, the rear fairing can be slid back to accommodate a pillion.

Wire wheels and twin front discs and drum rear are standard, but triple discs and alloy wheels are optional, as is a full fairing. Although it helps high-speed riding, the engine tends to overheat in traffic with the close-fitting body. If the performance of the bike is not up to requirements, a tuned version called the Arturo Magni Special, with special engine preparation on an 861cc unit by the company's famed developer, is available.

After that, a special 116bhp 1100cc version, the Grand Prix, with chain drive for lightness, is offered in Germany.

50   MZ 250 SUPA 5

The 250 Supa 5 is the top of the East German Motorradwerk Zschopau's range and like most machines from iron curtain countries is a practical rather than super sporty and good-looking machine. However, the MZ is a good performer and its appearance is very deceptive.

The bike is based on a large-looking (due to the amount of cooling fins) two-stroke single-cylinder engine which uses ordinary piston porting. The 243cc motor using mix of 50:1, produces 21bhp at

5350rpm and an impressive 19lb ft of torque at 4850rpm. Performance is to the order of an 80mph top speed, while acceleration from a start over a quarter mile takes 17.9secs. The little bike is surprisingly frugal and superior to most of its competitors, in that it can cover up to 80mpg.

Interestingly, the clutch is mounted on the engine side of the primary drive chain and this is felt when the bike is accelerated, for it holds its speed for a little longer, something that is rather disconcerting at first, even though it presents no problems.

Although performance is quite good, the brakes are not up to it at all, and the small drum at the front needs a very firm grip before it stops the bike in anger. However, with an enormously long (11in) rear brake lever acting on the same size brake at the rear there is the reverse problem. The rider can get so much leverage on it that it is extremely easy to lock the wheel altogether which gets rid of most of the retardation found. Liberal use of rubber mountings give the Supa a pleasant ride and negate the effects of single-cylinder vibrations while the seat, although not over padded, is nevertheless comfortable. The fuel tank looks odd in front of the seat, as it is much taller and not tailored in at all, but it does hold a generous 3.8gals which gives a range of an incredible 300 miles. The finish and looks of the MZ are strictly utilitarian, but the amount of standard equipment offered is, again, quite the reverse. There is a 12-piece tool kit along with a puncture outfit, chain link and hand-pump; a tachometer and rear-view mirror are also included in the price.

What does not look too attractive but is otherwise extremely worthwhile is the casing which covers the whole of the driving chain, so keeping dirt and grit off and extending the maintenance intervals and the life expectancy of the chain itself.

51 NORTON COMMANDO

The Norton Commando, before production ceased in the middle of 1977, was steeped in British tradition, being well made, fast, economical and almost racer-like in the handling stakes. However, time had caught up with the beast that had given the famous Norton four-stroke pushrod twin a new lease of life in 1967, just prior to the new tide of multi-cylinder 'superbikes' which effectively killed it off. The big Norton started off in 750cc guise, but was soon upped to 850 form in a bid to keep its performance competitive with the growing competition. In fact, the Commando had to adapt quite a lot just to stay alive, with the gearchange pedal placed on the left, opposite to the traditional right-hand side, to suit the Americans, along with the adoption of electric start, which later models proudly advertised on their side panels. Disc brakes, too, were part of the bike's specification even if older Nortons had managed well enough with drum units.

The Commando last appeared in Mark 3 guise and then was a well loved and excellent bike. With 58bhp and plenty of torque available from its 828ccs, it could reach 112mph and accelerate strongly from almost any speed in any of its four gears. There was an added bonus, too, and that was that the fuel consumption would be upwards of 40mpg, with almost 60mpg possible if the bike wasn't pushed too hard. Firing a Commando into life is not as easy as the side panel might suggest for, although able to restart the big twin with ease when hot, a cold start usually presents more problems. The technique needed is to have everything switched on and then to use the kickstarter while at the same time pressing the starter button. That way the starter motor helps take the strain out of kicking and so easing the low-compression motor over to fire. On its own, the starter will not guarantee a start and is a good way of getting the battery flat. However, a Norton owner will usually be quite happy to except things that way.

Once on the road, the bike will be transformed, for its frame is one based on the famous featherbed Norton which set new trends in handling in its day, and since the technology of the cycle hasn't progressed as much as that of the motor, the Norton is still streets ahead of most of the opposition.

With Norton-Villiers-Triumph (NVT) concentrating on Easy Rider mopeds and the Commando out of production, it was thought that big Nortons were a thing of the past. However, NVT had its mind, and money, on other sights: a monocoque-framed Wankel rotary of the equivalent of 1200cc. It was due for production in early 1979 with performance predicted that would not need improving to stay with the opposition.

130

52 QUASAR

The Quasar looks more like an eccentric styling exercise than a production motor cycle, but late 1977 did indeed see the unusual car-like two wheeler get into production from the company based near Bristol in the west of England. Everything about the Quasar is different from the normal concept of a bike and even the frame would seem more suited to a car.

Made from Reynolds 531 tubing, the frame features two overhead bars which support the Quasar's roof and also protect the rider in the event of the machine overturning. The engine of the bike is mounted under the steering head and is in fact the alloy straight-four water-cooled four-stroke as used in the small Reliant cars. Of pushrod-valve design, the 848cc engine produces 40bhp at 5500rpm and 46lb ft of torque at 3500rpm.

The Quasar uses the clutch and gearbox of the Reliant too, and a great deal of difficulty was encountered when trying to adapt the synchromesh unit to work in a bike manner. The finished machine has in fact two gear pedals, one above the other, and the upper is pressed to change up while the lower is pressed to change down; nothing at all happens if both are pushed at once, so there is no chance of ruining the gearbox that way. Naturally, as can be expected, the actual changes are more time consuming and positive than on a conventional bike. A final drive featuring a shaft is used but is quite separate from the swinging arm.

A standard suspension layout is used at the rear, while the front uses a leading swing arm on a pivoted fork so that braking stresses do not affect suspension movement. In reality, the Quasar has to be steered rather than banked to turn, but once learnt the procedure is quite simple.

The most striking thing about the bike is that it has an all-enveloping body of sleek and sharp design. A gentle line from above the front wheel goes upwards over the riders head, past a luggage locker, where it ends abruptly to give a squared-off back. The rider sits inside in an upright position with both legs and arms forward, something like a sports car. This means that although quite comfortable most of the time, gravitational pull will more severely affect him under braking, where on a normal bike the body is naturally balanced against it. A hammock is slung from the roof and so the riding position can be adjusted; in fact, a passenger can be carried at a pinch.

The obvious advantage of the Quasar is that it is well protected against the elements (there is even provision for a heater to blow warm air on the rider's hands), but what is not so apparently obvious is the machine's low centre of gravity and remarkable aerodynamics. Performance of the 650lb bike with standard engine is remarkable with a top speed of just on 100mph, and fuel consumption of around 70mpg. A turbocharged version has been in prototype form and it is hoped to put that into production.

The Quasar is a very well balanced machine and can corner at speeds that would make sceptics think again and wonder whether it is just an attention getter and more like the direction in which two-wheeled vehicles ought to be developed.

53   RICKMAN KAWASAKI

The Rickman brothers, Don and Derek, were at one time world class motocross riders on machines using their own frames and named Metisse, meaning mongrel bitch in Gallic. They set up their own factory in Hampshire, England, in 1962 and produced some excellent bikes for use both on the road and off. More recently, they have been busy manufacturing glassfibre bodies, top boxes and fairings which are marketed not only under various names of other outlets, but also under well known bike manufacturers' labels who hand out the work to Rickman Bros Ltd. As the accessory business built up, concentration of production was taken from the bike side, although the two brothers were too enthusiastic about their bikes to let the line stop completely.

They make chassis units for Honda and Kawasaki bikes, in both touring and café racer guise, with the most popular being the racer-like version with the 1000cc Kawasaki 'Z' engine.

The frame of the Rickman is fairly conventional in design and has no tricks, but is also very sturdy and well engineered. It is built of Reynolds 531 manganese molybdenum which when assembled is nickel plated. The finish is rather like chrome, except that it has a more golden tint to it. Lighter, stiffer and lower than the standard Kawasaki unit, the Rickman frame gives the bike more positive steering and far superior handling and, with famous Red Arrow Dunlop tyres, roadholding is excellent; braking is taken care of by three cast-iron discs mounted on attractive six-spoke alloy wheels.

The glassfibre bodywork of the bike can be purchased separately and fitted to a standard Japanese machine, and consists of a half-dolphin fairing, side panels, front mudguard, tank cover which fits over an alloy tank of 3.5gals capacity, and a tail/seat unit which can be either of single or double design. Handlebars are of clip-on type which with the rear set pedals and seat fitted well back give the rider a purely racing crouch riding position. Instruments are some of the few items apart from the engine that are taken from the standard Kawasaki bike. The others are the side and centre stands. Unfortunately, as the bike is a lot lower than standard, the centre stand is impossible to operate without help.

The Rickman has slightly lower gearing than standard, but this and a 40lb weight saving are all that affect straight-line performance. Top speed is roughly 130mph, while it will accelerate over a quarter mile from start in 12.1secs.

54   ENFIELD INDIA 350

The Enfield India 350 is a bike straight from the past which is still available today. For, back in the 1950s, Royal Enfield sold manufacturing rights of two of their bikes (a 175cc two-stroke and a 350cc four-stroke) to the Indian government who wanted a bike to mobilise their forces. The bikes were built in Madras and, in still almost the same form as then, they are built today.

Although somewhat crude to manufacturers and riders both east and west of its home country, the machine is popular enough for the Indian bike-riding populous, the Government and a small but thriving export market. In all, 11,000 or so Enfields are built each year. The bike uses a simple overhead-valve pushrod, single-cylinder, four-stroke engine of 346cc which produces a maximum of 18bhp at 5600rpm with its lowly 6.5:1 compression ratio. Powerful it may not be (although a top speed of just over 70mph should not be frowned upon), but frugal it is. Well over 70mpg should be possible in most conditions with the bike, while a figure nearer 90 will be achieved by those who use fuel sparingly. Acceleration, naturally, is leisurely but more than adequate to keep up with traffic in town; a four-speed gearbox is utilised.

Handling of the machine is surprisingly good, but there is one criticism and that is that the braking, like everything else, is as per 1950s British middleweight, and that compared with today's standards is not good. 6.5in drums front and rear cope with stopping the 350lb bike, but only just. Everything else is old, solid, reliable and sturdy, if not immaculately, finished. As a no-nonsense form of transport with character and a 'good old days charm', the Enfield 350 works well.

55   SEELEY HONDA

The Seeley company is a lot like Rickman, and Colin Seeley, like the Rickman brothers, has a great competition career behind him. The difference is that Colin was a side-car racer and at one time even looked after the production racing car side of the famous Brabham racing car company. However, during his time dabbling with three wheels and four, he made a succession of solo racers which were renowned for their excellent handling.

A lot of the thinking that went into those racers found its way into the Seeley Honda, the road bike he manufactures which is fitted with the four-cylinder CB750 engine.

Like the Rickman, the Seeley uses Reynolds 531 tubing for its construction but in this case is usually finished in attractive gloss white rather than nickel. The front of the frame does indeed resemble the Rickman in that it has a wide duplex cradle and bracing just above the exhausts. Standard Honda forks are used, however, which is probably the one weak point in the chassis set-up. Although a standard K series, or F1 or F2 engine is fitted as standard, an overbored 1000cc Seeley is also available, and the frame will easily stand up to the extra power. Full specification includes a four-into-two Jardine exhaust system, Lockheed brakes, S & W multi-rate dampers at the rear and the very expensive Lester alloy wheels, which are usually fitted with Dunlop Red Arrow covers.

A small nose fairing is fitted while the bars are flat rather than outright racer clip-on style. The most eye-catching feature of the bike is the fuel tank which holds a massive 5.5gals, enough to give the Seeley a touring range of well over 250 miles. Because of the large tank, no compromise has been made with the seating which is purely for the rider alone and has a large tail piece/fairing for support.

Naturally, the bike does not have to be clothed in such expensive trimmings, and many other items can be fitted to the base Seeley frame, which gives the rider all the advantages of a smooth and powerful Japanese engine with the manners of an excellent British chassis.

56 SUZUKI TS185

The Suzuki TS series is the company's range of two-stroke trail bikes which come in 100, 125, 250 and 185cc sizes. The 185 is typical of the range, being more an occasional trail bike than a serious full-time off-road conveyance.

The single-cylinder engine features an interesting induction system as used by Suzuki on their motocross world championship winning RM bikes, called the 'Power Reed'. Instead of being either piston ported or reed valve, the TS uses a combination of the two with the inlet tract split. One path goes straight to the cylinder, while the other goes via a reed valve to the crankcase. Timing of the piston port is mild to give the unit good torque characteristics at low engine speeds, while the reed-valve controlled crankcase port helps the engine breath more efficiently at higher speeds, so the bike should have good acceleration over the whole rev range. In practice, the 183cc power unit produces 17bhp at 6500rpm and 14lb ft of torque at 6000rpm, so the torque curve peaks quite near the maximum power figure. The torque does stay flat at lower speeds, however, and the bike's low speed acceleration is quite good. The top speed of the bike is a shade under 70mph, while it should return around 60mpg.

The suspension system of the TS185 is not as sophisticated as Yamaha's, but nevertheless works quite well, as it indeed should, again being based on the RM design. The rear set-up is the company's 'Tru-Trac' system with the coil spring damper units angled more horizontally than road units.

A lot of the bike's off-road performance is dictated by the tyres which have to cope with all weather performance on tarmac as well as trail blazing on the dirt, so they are something of a compromise and do not offer a great deal of grip in slippery conditions.

Also of compromise are the trimmings which would easily get broken or knocked off were the bike put down. However, that detracts from the TS185's sound design with its ample 9.1in ground clearance and long-travel suspension. While not as quick or as strong as many trail bikes offered, the 185 has its advantages with not too much power to get the rider into difficulty and not much weight (216lb) for him to pick up, and, for a novice rider, those points can be really important.

57 SILK 700S

Through no lack of talent and fertile minds, the British motor cycle industry was floundering by the late 1970s and, although designers could come up with plans for bikes that would have few peers from any country, a lack of money prevented them reaching fruition.

That is not the case with the Derbyshire-based Silk company, however, and they approach the 1980s with full order books and full design schedules. The machine produced is of 656cc two-stroke design and from the outside it looks like a latter-day Scott. One could be forgiven for that mistake for indeed the firm started off with a bike powered by an engine of that manufacture. Although it was not a great success on the race tracks, Silk thought that it would make an ideal roadster, but plans fell through with the owner of production rights to the Scott engine. The next best thing was for George Silk to build his own engine, which was to be of essentially the same design.

The power unit of the 700S is a two-stroke twin which is canted over forwards and which is liquid cooled. The large radiator is mounted forward of the engine and cooling is by the thermosyphon method which saves using a pump. Two-strokes are by nature very thirsty and dirty engines, but this has been cured to a large extent by the company's resurrection of Dr Schnuerle's loop scavenge system developed into a 'velocity contoured charge/scavenge' layout. It is essentially a complexly designed piston and port system which gets mixture into the combustion chamber more efficiently and gets it out again with the same vigour. It makes the bike cleaner and gives it an increase in low-to-mid-engine-speed torque as well as cures it of seemingly quenchless thirst. Maximum power of the single carburettor unit is 48bhp at 6000rpm, while maximum torque peaks well down at 3000rpm. The company do not quote specific torque figures, but the output is high for the maximum bhp figure corresponds to 42lb ft, which is remarkable. Being a two-stroke, the engine is quite light (a shade over 65lb) and this helps the bike's overall weight which is a miniscule 310lb. This along with a Spondon frame almost identical to that of their races, means that handling and roadholding of the Silk are of the highest order, while a disc at the front and drum at the rear stop the bike easily. Twin discs at the front or conical brakes of Campagnolo manufacture are also available, the latter built into Campagnolo alloy wheels. Other options available include panniers, top box and carriers, while Silk also have the patent on an ingenious centrally heated fairing.

If more performance is needed, a production racer is available, while the company is also developing a three-cylinder supercharged version of 1000cc.

58 SUZUKI X7

250cc motor cycles are popular largely because they are the biggest bikes available to learner riders and therefore it may seem to be a poor policy of Suzuki in advertising their 250cc X7 as a true 100mph machine, a point which will no doubt attract many novices to it. However, the X7 is a very good bike, and more than a match for bikes of almost twice its size.

The heart of the machine is a two-stroke air-cooled twin like its GT250 predecessors, the difference being that the X7 had adopted

the 'Power-Reed' induction of the TS trail-bike series, which boosts
torque at low to medium engine speeds. Maximum power is 29bhp
at 8000rpm which does indeed give the 278lb bike a top speed of just
on the magic 'ton', while acceleration over a quarter mile from
standing start is just outside of the 'fourteens', standing at 15secs
dead. As can be expected, the price one pays for performance from
such a small engine is fuel consumption and the X7 will return just
36mpg.

A six-speed gearbox is used which makes sure that the engine can
be kept spinning high up the range for maximum acceleration,
although the torque of the bike is so good that the front wheel can be
lifted with apparent ease without resorting to slipping the clutch.

The X7 is not intended as simply a drag-strip type roadster,
however, for a lot of thought has gone into the bike's chassis, so that
cornering too is sporting. The company advertises that the machine
has a banking angle of 45° on the left and 46° on the right, although
this will vary greatly on riders' weights; they assume the roads are
dry, too, for such cornering.

Although many smaller four-strokes have the luxury of electric
starting, the Suzuki just has a kick lever, but with a compression of
6.7:1 on a two-stroke that should be no hindrance at all.

Styling is very modern with carefully colour-keyed paintwork
with shiny and matt-black contrasting well with the basic scheme
and alloy wheels.

If the morals behind this '100mph learner' are debatable, Suzuki
on the other hand should be praised for their cunning in just having
'X7' on the bike's side panels, so giving it a certain mystique and
also saving the rider from letting on that his 'ton up' bike is a mere
250.

59   SUZUKI GS400

Suzuki have steadily developed their GS400 since it was introduced
in early 1977, and it has become a very sophisticated and well-
engineered middleweight machine.

The GS400 uses an air-cooled four-stroke engine which has twin
overhead camshafts, like the larger multis in the range, and which is

of 180° configuration. Drive for the camshafts is from between the cylinders on the crankshaft and the cam chain has the Suzuki Positensioner which, as its name implies, automatically keeps it at the right tension all the time. The engine produces maximum power at its redline of 9000rpm, a figure of 36.5bhp, while maximum torque of 23.9lb ft is produced at 7500rpm. The torque curve is quite interesting, for it more strongly resembles a horizontal straight line from around 3500rpm, with the figure just over 20lb ft all the way along. On the road, this makes the Suzuki a smooth and very responsive performer which is helped by the almost-universal-for-Japanese-four-stroke-twins balance system.

The bike has a six-speed gearbox which has a very slick and positive change and a virtually perfect set of ratios, although as the bike can easily reach maximum revs in top gear, a longer ratio would help cruising and ultimately fuel consumption. However, the efficient little engine makes the bike quite frugal anyway and it can quite easily cover over 60 miles on one gallon. Top speed of the GS is just over 100mph, while acceleration over a quarter mile from a standing start takes just under 16secs.

The flat bars on the bike make the riding position a little crouched and so uncomfortable around town, but they have the advantage of making it easier to exploit the machine's taut handling and good roadholding. Braking is by a single disc at the front (which is thinner than that of earlier models) and a drum at the rear which make light work of stopping the 380lb machine.

Styling of the GS400 is quite attractive with a neat seat/tail section under which is a small oddments tray and compartment in the rear. Instruments have the Suzuki orange glow at nighttime and there is the digital gear-position indicator which helps forgetful riders.

Not content with having the opposition produce similar bikes, in late 1978, Suzuki brought out a version with electronic ignition, alloy wheels and an overbored 425cc engine. The GS425 was, with its unique size, to run alongside the GS400 until 1979 when it would replace it.

Like Honda's bike which was uprated from 500cc, the Suzuki GS550 has a rather unusual engine size which the manufacturers hope will distinguish their multi-cylinder wares from the recent crop of half-litre twin-cylinder bikes which have appeared on the market. Of course, the extra capacity also gives a bonus of more performance and the GS550 has a very good turn of speed indeed. Like the larger 750 and 1000 Suzukis, the 550 has a four-cylinder air-cooled twin-overhead-camshaft power unit lying across the frame breathing through four carburettors. In this guise, the almost square engine (56 × 55.8mm bore and stroke) produces 51bhp at 9000rpm and 30lb ft of torque at 7500rpm. The power is transmitted through a six-speed gearbox (making the bike the largest capacity machine with as many ratios in production) and gives it a top speed of just over 110mph, while a standing start quarter mile can be covered in 13.7secs. Fuel consumption will work out at 45mpg. Although not as powerful as the larger multis in the Suzuki range, the bike has about 45lb less weight to carry so is more manageable in traffic and allows the rider to use the performance more.

With a smaller chassis, the GS550 is easier to handle on corners than its stablemates, although its ultimate roadholding will be roughly the same. However, the new generation Suzukis are among the best behaved bikes available and a long way from the machines that gave the Japanese industry the reputation for building sloppy and even dangerous bikes.

Braking is taken care of by two stainless steel discs at the front and a drum at the rear, which should make wet weather braking less nerve wracking. The instruments on the GS550 are excellent and radiate a warm orange glow at night time which is more pleasing to the eye than the usual green, while there is a neat digital gear-position indicator which glows red and which is certainly a help, as the smooth unfussed nature of the bike's engine makes it hard telling which of the many gears is selected.

The finish of the middleweight Suzuki is excellent and it comes with twin mirrors, pinstripe paintwork and an attractive four-into-two exhaust system.

61 SUZUKI GT750

The Suzuki GT750 was the only large two-stroke machine built with an accent on touring in the 1970s, even though a passing glance at its engine would have reminded you of something in a road-racing bike.

The heart of the big Suzuki is a three-cylinder triple which utilises liquid cooling and, from the outside, looks a lot like Suzuki's racer of the same capacity as used by Barry Sheene and team-mates in Superbike racing a couple of years ago which indeed did use the base 750GT motor. However, the GT's triple produces a 'mild' 70bhp at 6500rpm which is not enough for racing, but ample to push the surprisingly heavy (520lb) machine at quite high speed; a top of 122mph, in fact. In spite of the bulk, the GT's acceleration is brisk, too, and can reach 80mph from a standing start in just under 10secs.

One instinctively thinks of a two-stroke bike as being untractable by nature, but in the Suzuki's case nothing could be further from the truth, for the engine produces an enormous 61.5lb ft of torque at 5500rpm, which is a lot more than most other three-quarter litre bikes. This, along with the smoothness of a two-stroke and the quietness of a liquid-cooled engine, makes for an ideal tourer.

With the water jacketing, radiator and tall bars, the Suzuki looks cumbersome and ungainly and, compared with later models from the same company, the GT feels and handles that way, too. One benefit from its soft suspension, is the ride which is more comfortable than most on irregular surfaces, although the benefits of that disappear at the next corner where the bike wallows a little.

Braking is good with twin discs at the front and drum at the rear, although the discs do suffer in wet conditions, like most stainless steel units. Fuel consumption on a large 'stroker' would again be assumed as poor compared to a four-stroke, but in reality it averages out at a respectable 36mpg which is a lot better than two-stroke machines half its size manage at times.

The main failing with a two-stroke bike is that it is dirty and, even though it does not use a great deal of oil, the GT750 throws out a lot of smoke from its four tail pipes. That fact alone was enough to convince the manufacturers that the more complicated four-stroke was the best answer and so the four-cylinder air-cooled GS750 which ran alongside the GT for a while took over as the 750 of the late 1970s and early '80s.

62/63   SUZUKI RE5

Suzuki took on a big chance when they invested a vast amount of money on Felix Wankel's rotary engine, for they tooled up for a large production run and had to pay NSU a lot of money for the licence to build the unit. In the end, it was decided too late that the time was not right for the bike so everything was shelved in late 1977, just four years after the RE5 was launched.

Depending on your school of thought, the Wankel can be one of three capacities, but generally speaking the 497cc RE5 is equivalent to a 1000, being of single-rotor, three-chamber design. The motor sits in the frame with the eccentric shaft around which the engine rotates mounted crossways. Cooling and lubrication present problems and the bike has a wet slump which puts oil into the centre of the motor while there is a separate tank for the two-stroke oil for combustion. The lubricating oil passes through its own radiator, while due to the configuration, another radiator is needed for the liquid cooling. To add to that, there is a separate lubrication system for the gearbox. All in all, it adds a lot of weight to the bike and in some way detracts from one of the Wankel's advantages: simple layout and low weight. Also, in the RE5, smoothness and quietness of operation are not up to that achieved in NSU's Ro80 car, for example, and nowhere near as good as many four-stroke multis. However, the bike does have a fair amount of power with 62bhp at 6500rpm and, more importantly, 54.9lb ft of torque produced at a lowly 3500rpm and it does not drop off by a large amount until the engine is revving very near to its limit. In practice, such a wide power band means a more relaxed performance with less need for lots of gear changes. The RE5 has a top speed of 109mph, accelerates from a standing start over a quarter mile in 13.5secs but has a very poor fuel consumption.

Averaging out at just over 30mpg, the figure can drop to a little over 20mpg which is impractical even with a fuel tank which holds almost four gallons.

Along with the modern engine, the RE5 had space-age looks with, as its main attention grabber, matching instrument binnacle and rear light cluster, both being tubular in design. The instruments had a tinted perspex cover which, when the ignition key was inserted would slide back to reveal a speedometer, tachometer, water-temperature gauge and a multiplicity of warning lights. When the RE5 gave way to the updated RE5A, units similar to those on the GT750 took their place.

However, by the time the A version had appeared, the company from Hamamatsu had learnt its lesson and had shelved their rotary plans indefinitely, or until such times as the car manufacturers had pioneered their way with a second generation of Wankels and convinced the public that they are a viable proposition.

64 SUZUKI GS1000

The GS1000EC Suzuki looks a great deal like the smaller GS750 bike in the range, but underneath they are quite different machines indeed. Like its smaller stablemate, the 1000 uses an air-cooled four-cylinder four-stroke unit with twin overhead camshafts. However, as well as increasing the capacity of the engine to just over 997cc, they also took 10lb of weight from it by way of removal of the kickstarter, lighter crankshaft and different engine casting webs. In the rest of the bike, a further 25lb was added which is not a lot at all. So, the GS1000 has all the advantages of 1-litre power with none of the disadvantages of weight that is the bane of the other Japanese bikes in its class.

The engine produces 87bhp at 8000rpm and 61.3lb ft of torque at 6500rpm which gives the Suzuki a top speed of 136mph and enables it to accelerate over a quarter mile from standing start in 11.9secs. Fuel consumption is 44mpg. Where the bike has a significant advantage over the opposition is in handling, for the GS1000 has none of the frame flex that was so common with earlier bikes and its suspension is as advanced as any that is available, even on production Italian machines.

At the front, Suzuki use their race-proved air forks which are adjustable. A bicycle hand-pump is all that is needed to alter the pressure between 11 and 17psi to give either ideal travel for a solo rider on bumpy roads or high-speed cornering with two up and plenty of luggage: two extremes, but anywhere in between can be used. Advanced air/oil dampers are used at the rear which again are completely adjustable. Braking is by three 11in discs while standard cross-spoked-style Suzuki alloy wheels are used.

A five-speed gearbox, like that of the 750, is fitted but the larger bike does not have the luxury of that digital gear indicator. Another luxury that is missing is shaft drive, but the company were planning to bring out a machine of basically the same design with that form of final drive fitted.

Styling of the bike is middle-of-the-road and may even be considered quite ordinary with no gimmicks or any obvious aesthetic embellishments, but the bike is efficient and does everything as well as, if not better than, its competitors.

65 TRIUMPH TRIDENT

The Triumph Trident first appeared in 1968 and was the first of the modern day superbikes with more than two cylinders. Soon after, the BSA Rocket-3 was launched, being essentially similar to its one-time rival except that its engine was canted forward by 15°, while that of the Triumph was vertical. After the BSA company went under, Triumph decided that they would use the BSA-style engine in their Trident which, apart from putting more weight on the front wheel to improve handling, would also enable them to fit an electric starter: one point that stopped the British bike from having the all-round appeal of its Japanese competition.

The late Tridents were sophisticated models indeed and it was unfortunate that the British industry could not persevere with its development.

The T160 Trident has a 120° four-stroke three-cylinder engine which produces 58bhp at 7250rpm and more importantly an abundance of torque, so that it will pull strongly from low speeds in each of its five gears; another improvement over the earlier models which only had four ratios.

Even though the engine is rather dated in that it utilises pushrod and rocker valve actuation, the tuned exhaust note gives it a distinct charm, and also that famous British reputation of being unburstable. With the ability to sustain revving at engine speeds over 9000rpm without damage, it is easy to see where the reputation came from.

With a top speed of over 115mph, the Trident is only a little away from its rivals, while the acceleration is not quite in the four-cylinder Japanese class, and only just quicker than the twin-cylinder models of the same company. Fuel consumption, too, is not a strong point and in normal riding over 35mpg is difficult to achieve. Oil consumption on the other hand is better than one would expect of a British bike and, while it is in the engine, is cooled by a radiator mounted above the unit just under the steering head. Although quite heavy for a triple at 503lb, the Trident is amazingly agile and few manufacturers can boast of a frame that is equal to that of the Triumph in rigidity. The bike's singular discs at either end are also effective in both wet and dry and make light work of stopping from high speed repeatedly.

The large Triumph is a good looking machine with its siamesed exhaust running from the centre cylinder and then splitting to by-pass the single down tube of the frame on either side, and it is a great pity that NVT or the Meriden Co-Operative had no room for it in their schedules. Although in latter years its performance was eclipsed by foreign opposition, it perhaps sums up the British industry when it was said that Triumph could not afford to develop their overbored prototype 850cc Trident.

66/67 TRIUMPH BONNEVILLE

The Triumph Bonneville, like the Norton Commando, has been part of British biking for many years, but it still appeals to riders who are not impressed with multi-cylindered sophisticated machinery and would rather settle for a well-bred 'iron' which can trace its parentage back many generations, something Japanese bikes can't do just yet.

The specification sheet of the latest Bonneville from the workers' co-operative at Meriden looks a little better compared to its foreign opposition, but is still rather dated.

The heart of the 'Bonny' is a parallel-twin engine of 744cc. Valve actuation is by pushrods and rockers and is fed by two Amal concentric carburettors which have built-in starting jets, and which conform to American regulations. Previously, to start the bike, a float chamber tickler had to be pressed until the unit flooded and only then could a hefty swing on the kickstarter fire the 7.9:1 compression ratioed engine to life. That is a thing of the past now, and only the big kick is needed.

The main modification over the older Bonnevilles is the adoption of electronic ignition which makes the bike faster, cleaner and more frugal; an uprated alternator, with more power at low engine speeds and a change from positive to negative earth. Power from the engine is unchanged and it produces 50bhp at 6200rpm and a useful amount of torque. The bike's top speed is 112mph, while fuel consumption is a little low for a British twin at 45mpg. The design of the Triumph engine may be a bit dated, but the gearbox is as smooth and light to use as any other bike; five ratios are used.

The chassis of the Triumph is excellent and with Dunlop tyres, Lockheed brakes (single disc at either end) and low 395lb weight, it is at home on the twistiest of roads.

The latest bikes have revised instrumentation and, although not nearly in the same class as the excellent Japanese units, are a great improvement over pre-1979 Triumphs. The finish of the machines is excellent and the pin-striping of the tank is all done by hand and far superior to any masked paintwork or transfers. The Bonneville comes in two versions: standard with flat bars and four gallon tank or 'US spec' with high rise bars and a smaller but more shapely three gallon tank. The 1979 models have reverted to chrome mudguards, too.

68   YAMAHA RD250

Although the Aermacchi-Harley-Davidsons and Kawasakis have recently been reaping the rewards on the race tracks in the 250cc class, Yamaha has produced many World Championship winning bikes and still produces machines for no less than 90% of the riders.

Their road-going two-stroke RD250 bears a strong resemblance to its brother racers, even though it is air rather than liquid cooled. The 54×54mm bore and stroke twin-cylinder engine produces 32bhp at 8000rpm with its lowly 5.8:1 compression and pushes the bike to a top speed of 92mph. Like the racers, the RD uses reed-valve induction which is claimed helps fuel consumption, and it returns 44mpg, although this is increased drastically if the engine is kept revving at a high rate.

The late model RD250s have six-speed gearboxes which is an improvement over the older versions' five. Interestingly, the earlier bikes had six gears in the housing but the highest one was blanked off, although it could be put into use after a strip down.

The handling of the RD again is akin to their racers and it is quite happy being thrown into bends at high speeds, something which is helped by its 340lb weight. Stopping, too, is easy with a disc brake at either end. Unlike Yamaha's four-stroke 250, the XS, the two-stroke model has no electric starter, but the low-compression engine is easy enough to crank over by hand, and is quite fuss free and willing to tick over without fouling its plugs, something that was definitely not the case with many 'strokers' of the 1960s.

The other large two-stroke roadster built by Yamaha is the RD400 which is basically the same except for the engine capacity and, with around 8bhp more and just 11lb extra weight, is a real flier and even more like the track bikes which share the same colour schemes.

69   YAMAHA DT250 ENDURO

The Enduro/Trail bike is a phenomenon of the 1970s, with the machine built purely for fun and the fact that it can be used as an everyday commuter an added bonus.

The Yamaha DT250 is typical of the breed and, although it has all the equipment necessary to make it road legal, it uses sensible fittings to ensure that it doesn't get damaged in tumbles on the rough.

The power unit for the DT250 is a single-cylinder, two-stroke which uses a reed valve for induction. This is a device with two stainless steel plates which are mounted in such a way that the engine with its 'suction' on the downward stroke will take in the right amount of mixture then, on the upward stroke, the pressure from compression and the natural springiness of the valves will shut so that mixture will not get in, thus avoiding the waste of usual piston-port two-stroke units. Yamaha have had great success in both motocross and road racing with their reed-valve engines.

The DT250 is not in a high state of tune like the competition bikes, however, and produces just 23bhp at 6000rpm, with the optimum torque produced at 500rpm less. This means that full use has to be made of the five-speed gearbox to keep the bike in its narrow power band. The engine is mounted in a high narrow frame which gives ten inches of ground clearance and, even if you have to make full use of it, there is a metal guard to protect the sump; helping in this respect too is the exhaust system which runs up and over the engine to exit level with the top of the rear wheel.

The frame itself is based on another famous Yamaha trademark, the cantilever monoshock unit where, instead of having two spring/damper units on either side running from the hub to the top of the frame, the DT has a whole subframe, which pivots where a trailing arm would be, to work a single large damper which rests in the top tube of the frame. The whole unit allows greater wheel travel for given suspension movement. It makes little or no difference on the road, but the benefits are felt if the bike is treated to its full potential on the rough.

The practical off-road capability is accentuated by the rubber-covered instruments, the indicators which are on rubber stalks and the plastic mud guards which don't shatter when the bike is dropped as often happens with fun riding on the trails.

70/71   YAMAHA SR500

Off-road bikes are usually of single-cylinder design and in Motocross Grands Prix, the norm is two-strokes of 400–440cc and four-strokes of around the half-litre mark. In recent years, the Japanese manufacturers have built similar trail bikes and, just like their competition counterparts, have too grown steadily in size. Yamaha produced the biggest of the lot with their XT500 four-stroke 'thumper' and suddenly everyone saw a lot more than an off-road bike. They remembered with fondness bikes like the BSA Gold Star and soon magazines expressed interest in project road bikes built around the Yamaha engine/transmission. Yamaha themselves took the hint and produced the SR500 saying that this was an obvious way to go as there was no new ground to break with turbine-like multis. Whatever the reason, the wheel had turned full circle and a new generation could savour the delights (and curses) of 'the big single'.

The SR500, in true Japanese fashion, is a well engineered bike and in most places the toil of owning such a machine has been developed out: like leaks, dubious electrics and general lack of reliability. The machine is powered by an oversquare engine of 499cc with valve actuation by a single overhead camshaft. Essentially the same alloy unit as the XT off roader, the SR differs in valves size and port shape so is a little more potent. A maximum power figure of 33bhp at 6500rpm is not a lot for a 500, but peak torque is just over 28lb ft at 5500rpm, and indeed the torque curve is remarkably flat from 2000rpm to that figure. A five-speed gearbox is used and the bike will reach a top speed of just on 100mph in the highest of them. Fuel consumption is a bonus feature of such a bike and the SR500 should have no difficulty in producing an overall figure of well over 50mpg.

Rather than try to get a starter to turn over a 500cc cylinder with a 9:1 compression ratio, Yamaha decided to leave firing to a hefty rider, although they do make it as easy as possible. A compression release lever is fitted and the engine is turned carefully so that the piston is at the top of its stroke. A little window on the camshaft cover indicates when this point has been reached. The bike should then fire at the first kick. A vacuum automatic advance and retard system (like that of the XS1100) also helps. Also dispensing with an electric starter helps save weight as again a plus point of a single is that it is quite light. Dry weight of the machine is 348lb so a single disc brake at the front and drum rear ably stop it. Handling is good, too, and the narrow bike instils a lot of confidence in the rider to make full use of it.

The SR500 Yamaha may not suit everyone, but it does take the tears out of 'vintage biking'.

72 YAMAHA XS400

Like Kawasaki, Yamaha have been trying to cater for all tastes and marketing machines with similar capacity in both two-stroke and four-stroke guises. The XS400 is the company's four-stroke machine in the popular 400 class and is completely different from the RD400 two-stroke which has a much sportier image, even if in reality both bikes are just about equal in performance.

The XS400's nearest relation is the similar-looking 250, and both have parallel air-cooled twin-cylinder engines driving through six-speed gearboxes. The single-overhead-camshaft unit is very oversquare with dimensions of 69mm bore by 52mm stroke, and it can rev to 9000rpm, which is quite high for a twin. Unlike the other 400 twins in the same class, the XS does not have counter balance shafts, which means the motor does vibrate more than the opposition, but this is not noticeable above 4500rpm. More important than the bike's 38bhp is the torque produced which peaks at 22lb ft at 7500rpm, but stays within 5lb ft of that figure right down to 4000. On the road, this means that the Yamaha will pull strongly and evenly over a large speed band. A top speed of 101mph can be achieved while acceleration over a standing start quarter mile takes a very creditable 14.9secs. There are single disc brakes at either end to stop the bike which are mounted on attractive alloy wheels which, in turn, help take away some of the bulkiness of the bike's looks. Yamaha have also devised neat paintwork on the tank and side panels which helps break up the lines, again to make the bike appear smaller than its 362lb would otherwise suggest.

The standard of equipment on the middleweight Yamaha is equal to that of many Japanese machines, and betters them with an ingenious indicator system which is worked by a linkage to the speedometer. This means that the winkers stay on for a certain distance which has no bearing on time but just distance travelled.

The indicator switch can be simply pressed inwards to override the unit.

73   YAMAHA XS500

Although looking like the smaller XS400 and XS250 bikes, the XS500 has a different twin-cylinder engine which features twin-overhead camshafts and four-valves per cylinder.

Although such an engine would be ideally suited to a sports motor cycle, Yamaha instead have used it in a state of tune for a bike they classify as a tourer with enough engine power to enable it to keep up with larger capacity machines.

The oversquare power unit displaces 498cc and with a compression ratio of 9.6:1 produces 49bhp at 8500rpm, just one brake horsepower down on the company's 650cc twin. A four-valve-per-cylinder engine is used because four small valves use space more efficiently than two larger valves, so that, in fact, more head area can be utilised which in turn makes the engine more efficient. Also the lower reciprocating mass of small valves means higher engine speed before 'bounce' is induced, and better ignition is helped by the sparking plug being central in the head, its most efficient position. The problem with the layout is that to get the valves in an efficient semi-hemispherical head, twin overhead camshafts have to be employed or a complicated system of pushrods and rockers which would negate the effect of the extra engine speed gained from the layout. The XS uses direct-operating overhead cams which make servicing more complicated and time consuming.

The Yamaha has pistons set at 180° unlike many four-strokes with their 360° layout with the inherent vibration difficulties. However, Yamaha had the problem of the crankshaft rocking with the alternate reciprocation, so to encounter this they use their patented 'omniphase' balance shaft.

The top speed of this 425lb bike is 105mph, while it will accelerate over a quarter mile from standing start in 14.3secs; fuel consumption is 46mpg. In all, the XS500 is deceptive for it is more advanced than it looks and 'four-stroke twin' specification suggest. However, although the engine is efficient and powerful, the extra complication of the valve gear means more complicated and expensive maintenance.

74 YAMAHA XS1100

When Yamaha announced their XS750 three-cylinder four-stroke, it was acclaimed as an excellent tourer with the best shaft drive of any machine available. If one thing was lacking it was outright performance for, although quick, it could not match the top-of-the-range models of the other Japanese manufacturers. The obvious idea would have been to graft an extra cylinder on the 750 to make it a 1000, but Mitsui Machinery decided to go one better and so the XS1100 was born.

The engine of the bike is an air-cooled unit of just a shade under 1102cc and, with its valves actuated by twin overhead camshafts, produces 95bhp at 8000rpm and 66.5lb ft of torque at 6500rpm. The whole unit is canted forward a few degrees and an oil cooler just under the steering head helps keep the motor running cool. Chain and gear primary drive goes to a wet-multi-plate gearbox and thence to a five-speed gearbox and the shaft drive which runs along the left side of the bike. The gear lever pedal is pivotted at the front so that it looks back-to-front but it does work in the normal one-down-four-up sequence.

Top speed of the big Yamaha is 138mph, while it will accelerate to a quarter mile from a standing start in just under 12secs; fuel consumption is 41mpg. The most awe-inspiring thing about the XS1100 is its size and mass, for it dwarfs just about everything apart from Harley-Davidsons. Once travelling at a few mph and the weight is forgotten, but it does affect the high-speed handling of the bike and the braking. Even though the Yamaha uses three 11.23in diameter discs, they are not up to stopping the 564lb bike repeatedly from high speed, although the 3.5in front and 4.5in wide rear tyres keep their grip.

Although the Yamaha has a sprint-like turn of speed, it is primarily intended for touring as its high bars and 5.28gal fuel tank prove. Not having to adjust the chain every 150 miles or so is a boon for long-distance travel, too.

The styling of the XS1100 is rectangular, with headlight, instruments, indicators and reflectors all this rather odd-looking shape.

Standard equipment on the bike includes fuel gauge, a cut off switch for the ignition should the bike fall over, self-cancelling indicators and sockets for intercom, fog lamps or other accessories that might be fitted.